The Ministry of the Christian Wife

RIBBING HIM & RIGHTLY

Beneth Peters Jones

Second Edition

 **BJU PRESS**

Greenville, SC 29614

Library of Congress Cataloging-in-Publication Data

Jones, Beneth Peters, 1937-
   Ribbing him rightly: the ministry of the Christian wife/ Beneth Peters Jones.--2nd ed.
   p.cm.
   ISBN 1-57924-406-8
   1. Wives-Religious life. 2. Christian women--Religious life. I Title.
BV4528.15 .J67 2000
248.8'435--dc21

                                                  00-041438

Note: The fact that materials produced by other publishers may be referred to in this volume does not constitute an endorsement by Bob Jones University Press of the content or theological position of materials produced by such publishers. The position of Bob Jones University Press, and of the University itself, is well known. Any references and ancillary materials are listed as an aid to the reader and in an attempt to maintain the accepted academic standards of the publishing industry.

All Scripture is quoted from the Authorized King James Version.

Ribbing Him Rightly
Second Edition

Cover and design by Jamie Leong
Composition by Agnieszka Augustyniak and Beata Augustyniak

Dedication

For *Bob—beloved husband, dearest friend, and patient endurer of this oft-failing "rib" for forty years.*

꼿

Contents

Acknowledgments

My special thanks to the women confidantes who convinced me I'm not the only oft-crumbling wifely rib, and to Jean Saito, M.D., who kindly served as technical consultant in the matter of physical ribs.

Introduction

Ribbing Him Rightly

Why that for a title? First, obviously, the title alludes to woman's creation when God took a rib from man's side. Second, as far as we wives go, there are ribs, and then there are ribs. (To be perfectly honest, most of us must confess that even within ourselves as individuals we are not the same kind of rib from one day to the next.)

"Yes, but," you may ask, "why another book on marriage?" As a general rule, secular publications ignore the spiritual, downplay the practical, and exalt the physical and psychological. Christian books are, of course, more

helpful; still, many of the authors (intentionally or otherwise) purport to be honey-and-
peaches wives—and from that pinnacle of
doubtful perfection they speak.

But what about those of us whose humanity grits the honey and bruises the
peaches? It gets mighty rough down here in
the trenches of marital reality. So often, it's
not the big things that defeat us, but the
seemingly insignificant, seldom-voiced, little
things. Numberless wives have poured into my
ears their stories of disappointment in themselves and their husbands, of frustration over
the conflict between godly desire and unholy
reactions, of confusion over the exact nature
and boundaries of their responsibilities. It is
to and for *us* the marital mortals, this book is
undertaken.

In Ribbing Him Rightly I intend to
write candidly, practically, and woman-to-
woman. Furthermore, God's Word must be
basic in *any* approach to marital relationships,
for without it marriage becomes both a trial
and a travesty. Also, anyone dealing with marital trials cannot lose sight of her sense of
humor, for surely marriage not only offers situations humorous in themselves, but it also

Aye, There's the Rib!

has some in which a woman knows she'd *better* laugh—or else she'll cry!

So much for explanations and introduction. Now, let's get on into this business of right ribbing.

§

Chapter One

Aye, There's the Rib!

There he sits. A full-grown male of the species Homo sapiens who fills his days with the larger matters of human life, such as holding down a job (or trying to keep himself occupied in retirement), providing financial and physical security for a family, or stepping out in leadership of his own little flock. Impressive. This creature at whom we gaze is, according to advertisement and demonstration, independent, competitive, self-sufficient, strong-willed, and logical. This, then, in a word, is your husband.

Acknowledging the above observations to be true, we proceed logically to the question:"What am *I* doing here?"*I*, also classified as Homo sapiens, who claims no further similarities to the observed being?

Simply put, wife, you're here to be *that fella's rib.* Behind the observable facts just noted, there are many more aspects of your husband that make your existence and function necessary. You see, he is incomplete without you.

Who says? God says. In the very first book of His forever-settled, holy Word, the Bible, God explains the creation of woman.

On the sixth day of creation, the earth's newly formed occupants stood on tiptoe and held their breath as God declared His intention to give yet one more creation—man—to the infant earth. Made from earth's material itself, he was yet given rulership over all that had been made earlier.

So for a space of time man walked, and beheld, and named, and ruled—yet the completeness, the beauty seen on every hand stirred but failed to satisfy an inexpressible emptiness within his own being.

Of all the Creator's works, only this one, man, was pronounced "not good"—because of his isolation. "I will make him an help meet for him." To Adam, then, God brought a deep sleep from which would come a waking dream. Anesthetized by divine grace, Adam yielded up a portion of his own body, which would be remolded to an exquisite difference/likeness that God would return to him for

> *Woman as wife can be seen as both magnet and magnifier.*

unity more sweet, more full of meaning, than ever was the undivided body. As Adam woke to behold creation's crowning handiwork, he exulted first in her fulfilling existence: "This is now bone of my bones, and flesh of my flesh." Then in her identity: "She shall be called Woman, because she was taken out of Man."

And God Himself proclaimed: "Therefore shall a man leave his father and his mother, and shall cleave unto his wife: and they shall be one flesh."

In that divine statement, woman as wife can be seen as both magnet and magnifier. As magnet she draws man from his parental nurturing to the challenging maturity that establishes a new home. As magnifier she completes and expands him: she makes him whole.

Our infinitely wise God works in meticulous order. He moves in such a way that even the seemingly insignificant has manifold intricacies and applications. Have you ever wondered why a rib was God's choice for His creation of woman? The material intimates the function He intends. But what are ribs per se? A glimpse into their quiet but important existence may help to direct our thinking about wifely roles.

First, and most obviously, ribs are *bone*. Bone: the hard material in the human body. That structurally necessary framework upon which the physical system is suspended.

Ribs make up the thorax: the rigid-yet-flexible cage containing the principal organs of respiration and circulation and sheltering part of the abdominal organs. So, then, ribs provide support and protection for some supremely important parts of human anatomy.

Ribs do not just exist in the body in isolated splendor. They are tied in to the overall system. For instance, ribs are intricately connected to muscles. The large muscle called the diaphragm (chief muscle of breathing) attaches at its edges to the lower ribs. Numerous smaller muscles that lend flexibility and movement to the body, as in the case of arms, back, and abdomen, also tie into the ribs. Still other rib-connected muscles make possible the expansion and contraction of the chest as needed for inhalation and exhalation.

Ribs are also connected to the overall physical system via the nerve-and-blood network. Besides affording protection for the heart and its large veins and arteries, each rib is itself serviced by a nutrient artery and numerous blood vessels. In fact, because ribs are bone, they actually contribute to blood composition. Both red and white blood cells are manufactured in the center, or marrow, of bones, and from there pass into the bloodstream. Every rib also has its own nerve, which receives and sends messages vital to the body's well-being.

These greatly simplified facts about ribs—their composition, importance, and function—form the groundwork for later chapters in this book. I hope they stir you to consider personally the implications of God's choosing a rib as His basic material for wife-construction. My own study of ribs has convinced me that the Creator's *heart* was involved in His choice and that we wives can receive both instruction and inspiration from that choice.

શ્ચ

Chapter Two

Ribbing a Man

Ribs are bones with flexibility built into them. One of the marvels of God's creation in our physical bodies is His combining of apparent opposites—in this case, rigidity with flexibility. Ribs are far from being the largest bones in our bodies. At the same time, they must withstand considerable stress and pressure.

We wives are early—and continually—called upon to demonstrate both strength and flexibility. The first demand comes as the illusion of marriage becomes the reality of marriage. Fictional ideas of "love at first sight" and "they lived happily ever after" are so distorted that new wives are often shocked and disappointed by marriage's actuality.

We would be wise to set aside fantasy and accept fact. Marriage is simply a continued, more intricate form of life—and who would deny the problems and pressures of living? Yet romanticism persists in telling us that matrimony is a magical cure-all, a rose-hued land free of thorns and storms. And we want to believe the fairy tale.

Courtship adds to the illusion. While dating, both boy and girl exhibit their best behavior, their most pleasant personality, their most polished manners. But within the familiarity of marriage, they soon revert to comfortable behavior, true personality, and careless manners.

While big-heartedly excusing ourselves for our own shortcomings, we resent our husband's failure to be the Prince Charming our prenuptial eyes beheld. Some days, in some ways, we see him considerably more like a frog—unkissed and definitely unprinced! A woman must *adjust*—demonstrate flexibility—to the mutual nonroyal status.

About the time she's awaking from romantic dreams, a wife also becomes acutely aware of the fact that this creature to whom she has pledged herself for life is a man. Surprising as it may seem, a husband's simple maleness can cause his wife reactions that range from disbelief through dismay and into disgust.

Why and how can masculinity throw a woman into such a tizzy? By its difference from femininity! Contrary to the silly claims that men and women differ from each other only in inconsequential, environmentally produced ways, *we are as unlike as night and day!* The immensity of the difference does not fully dawn upon a woman until after marriage.

> *God's intention in creation was to form two different, yet complementary beings.*

We know the Bible says, "Male and female created he them" (Genesis 5:2)—but we've hurried over those familiar words without thinking about what they really mean. God's intention in Creation was to form two different, yet complementary beings.

Since junior or senior high school days, you've known that at conception the father's sperm determines the sex of the baby. The combination of the "X" chromosome

from the mother plus "X" from the father results in a girl, while the mother's contributed
"X" joined by the father's "Y" results in a boy.
But beyond the wonder of that creative miracle lies the fact that even in our most basic
structural components men aren't like women
and women aren't like men! The further science looks, the more distinctions it finds. For
instance, a man's blood has more red corpuscles than a woman's; his system is thereby sup-
plied with greater strength and stamina. He
has thicker skin than she—hence better insu-
lation and fewer wrinkles. His skeleton, especially in the region of pelvis and hips, is
differently constructed: his bones are not designed for childbearing! And so it goes—differences apparent in almost any comparison
of men with women.

To this point in the discussion, the
differences are little more than interesting.
Now let's consider a few areas in which a wife
might react negatively to her husband's maleness.

First, he doesn't think in the same way
she does. Science has discovered that our
brains actually function differently: men's
brains are right-hemisphere oriented, whereas
women's brains operate primarily from the

left hemisphere. Among other things, this difference means that men are logical and long-range in their thinking, while women are more detail-oriented and intuitive. Brain differentiation molds our most ordinary daily experiences as well as the crisis points; it also influences communication. We observe, analyze, and react to virtually everything *from opposite perspectives*. When the "bridge" between the two minds stubbornly resists completion, a wife is tempted to wail, "I just don't understand the way he thinks!" That is technically true. But instead of feeling frustration, discouragement, and anger, we can rejoice in recognizing what glorious opportunity God has given us even in our brain orientation to be completers! The Lord meant for husband and wife to interlock in every way: his logic balancing her intuition; his long view compensating for her attention to minutiae, and vice versa. But happy interlocking calls for flexibility.

A second trouble spot caused by male-female unlikeness lies in differing life focus. A woman's world consists primarily of marriage, home, and family. That is not true of a man. Although he values those things, the real emphasis of his life is his work. Does he deliberately operate that way to make his wife miserable? No! His life focus *was given him of God.* After Adam and Eve had forfeited Eden and begun the sad, sinful walk toward death, "the Lord God sent him forth from the Garden of Eden, to till the ground from whence he was taken" (Genesis 3:23). To the fallen Eve, God said, "Thy desire shall be to thy husband" (Genesis 3:16). The dichotomy of focus probably served as a thorn for Eve as soon as Eden's gates clanged shut behind the pair. It continues to prick us women to the present day.

The male concentration on occupation has a strange effect on some wives. It bends their attitude all out of shape, and they begin verbal husband punching: when he goes to work, when he comes home, when he makes phone calls about his work, when he reads books pertaining to it, and when he talks about his occupation. Such treatment, obviously, makes trouble. The wife is not enhancing her value to her husband; though perhaps more *aware* of her, he is not happily so. He feels discomfort over something he cannot alter. Nor is she helping herself. Her continued examination, discussion, and accusations only etch the matter more deeply in her mind, and she becomes increasingly unlovely and unlovable, even to herself.

Unhappily, there are some husbands who pursue their careers so single-mindedly that they neglect wives and children. But even that unbiblical extreme is not cured by a wife's complaining. The case of the truly neglectful husband should be taken to God's throne room, with the judgment and the solution turned over to Him.

There may be a few women reading this little book who don't identify with the "job competition" problem. Bless you. But most of us have battled the monster at one time or another; some may be in its clutches right now. Whether the attack be vicious and long-lived or mildly spasmodic, it can be countered by Proverbs 9:13: "A foolish woman is clamorous: she is simple, and knoweth nothing."

Gulp! Is *that* what I am? Yes, if I create clamor over an unchangeable male characteristic. How much better if we would ask the Lord's help in this troublesome area. The Spirit-controlled woman accepts and adapts to her husband's occupational bent, realizing that in this respect, too, she and he are to be complements. Even if she is a working wife, a woman's life centers in the globe of her home; a husband's existence is more like a constellation including the globe of home. Both are needed, right, and beautiful.

A third trouble spot is that created by the male-female difference: a man may not have the neatness or the sensitivity a woman has. Some of you are thinking, "Of course not!" But others are murmuring, "You said it, Lady! My husband's approach to life is like the proverbial bull in a china shop. He's sloppy and . . ." Hold it! Before building a case against him, consider . . .

A man's performance in life is unlike a woman's because *he* is unlike a woman. Delicacy in a man is out of place. Would you like to see graceful gestures from a man? Certainly not! They would mark him as effeminate. The same is true of delicacy in other areas. For instance, some wives complain about their husbands' less-than-neat habits. If messiness characterizes your husband, it may spring from one of two things: poor home training or his maleness. Note that the latter does not have housekeeper instinct built into it as does femaleness. The point is, why insist that he do things the way you do? Better far simply to accept the distinctives. If you had

wanted to live with women, you should have
stayed in a college dormitory the rest of your
life! As you accept the "He is male" concept,
learn to delight in all the marvelous differences between you: differences that allow the
two of you to interlock.

When you are tempted
to be resentful because
you have to do the
picking-up-after or the
details-catching or
whatever, remind yourself that those things
point to his need of you. After all, if a man naturally performed well in areas where we
females excel, as we sometimes wish, he
wouldn't need a wife, now would he?

> *Learn to delight in all the marvelous differences between you.*

A man's coarser self can also stand as
a reminder of our essential feminine refinement. As my husband puts it, "Woman is dust
twice refined." God made Adam from dust,
but He made Eve from Adam. That extra step
away from earthiness should be consistently
evident in women. But look what the Devil is
doing: he's tearing feminine refinement to
shreds. And as far as the world is concerned,
he has pretty well succeeded. Unisex and
"women's liberation" have induced women to
carve the bone of their being into a saw-toothed

knife! Most unfortunately, God's women have become susceptible to coarsening too. Every Christian woman ought to bear the hallmark of ladylikeness: that admirable quality of femininity that counterbalances the admirable quality of masculinity.

A wife's behavior ought to have the effect of smoothing out the rough edges on her man, not by criticism, but by her ladylike qualities that encourage the latent gentleman within the male breast. For the Christian woman, ladylikeness might be defined as a genteel manner arising from her "meek and quiet spirit." When women cease to be ladies, men abandon their gentlemanliness.

As I wrote the first draft of this book, our daughter, Roxane, was in the pre-engagement stage of courtship. As we were working together one evening preparing supper, she told me of an "experiment" she had undertaken with her boyfriend the last couple of days. She had deliberately restrained her independence in such things as removing or putting on a coat, opening doors, and picking up her books to carry them. She had then watched the masculine responses. She summed up the results of her experiment with, "It's really true—men *do* want to be gentlemen,

don't they?" They certainly do! That's a part
of masculinity: protectiveness and helpfulness
toward femininity. But many times that gen-
tlemanly quality starves to death while waiting
for a lady to honor and assist.

A fourth characteristic of maleness is
immaturity. As someone has accurately put it,
within every man lurks a seven-year-old boy.
Upon marriage, the female of the species
quickly changes from girl to woman; the male
changes from boy to man only *in part*. His
shoulders broaden to carry the multiplied
burdens of family support; his muscles harden
to enable him to face the workday world; his
mind takes on an intentness and acuity he
had no need for in youth. Yet somewhere deep
within his core of self, he stays forever boy-
like.

This little-boy characteristic has two
outstanding manifestations. The first is his
love for play. The man who would blush to
play with toy cars avidly follows the race car
circuit via TV, newspaper, and magazine. The
fellow who hung away his Little League cap
long years ago sits spellbound through numberless televised baseball, football, and/or bas-
ketball games. The guy who laughingly admits
to having watched Buck Rogers when he was a

kid now hangs around airports and is a walking encyclopedia of aircraft information. The little boy who delighted in dismantling his toys now spends hours in the garage tinkering on a truck, car, or motorcycle. And the list could go on.

The omnipresent masculine play complex baffles a woman. If *she* doesn't waste time in immature pursuits, why should *he*? The problem is that you can't compare apples with oranges! Women move into mature responsibility with little need for residual immaturity. Men, apparently, continue to have that need. Perhaps the zone of play is a necessary buffer against the greater burden of responsibility, of head-to-head competition the man experiences. And let's face it: we wives sort of blend our responsibility and our play, don't we? Yes, it is necessary to prepare meals, yet in doing so we know the fulfillment of creativity and the simple pleasure of providing the needs of those we love. Yes, financial conditions may demand home-tailoring our own and the children's clothes, but the process provides quiet, constructive enjoyment. Again, I believe the difference lies in God's assignment of distinctive roles. Man's "sweat of his brow" orientation demands some off-setting play, whereas woman's proper orientation offers in itself greater variety, enjoyment, and fulfillment. Both must have this balance.

When considering this matter of residual boyhood, the woman who rightly ribs her man will be tolerant. She'll neither scold nor scorn. She'll adapt and adore: adapt by backing off and giving him room to pursue his play; adore the little boy who peeps through even when he has gray in his sideburns. If you've been one (as I often have!) to deride the male play syndrome, replace the littleness of your attitude with the bigness of loving tolerance. A shining example of such tolerance came from a woman who attended a seminar a number of years ago. After one of the sessions, she came to the speaker's stand and shared this story of triumph:

"For years I gave my husband fits over his love of trucks. His time and attention and tinkering grated on me because it seemed he was always out in the yard working on a truck. Finally, I realized my nagging, pouting, and complaining were driving us *both* crazy. So I backed off and shut up. Now, when I want to talk to him, I just go out and crawl under the truck with him. You can't imagine how much our marriage has improved."

Ribbing Him Rightly

The second manifestation of a man's little boyness comes in his times of illness. Fast-blooming maturity makes a wife realize that sickness is just something to be treated, endured, and sometimes even ignored as she goes on about the business of daily living. Not so for a man. The sickness scenario, only slightly exaggerated, reads like this: A germ meanders your husband's way; he is devastated. A cold and sore throat become the backdrop for a performance rivaling *King Lear* for pathos. Should there be a degree or two of fever accompanying an illness, an onlooker would swear his bedridden, groan-punctuated state is terminal.

We wives tend to view this indication of immaturity with impatience, if not disgust. "How can a two hundred-pound man possibly carry on so over a microscopic, temporary invader?" we fume. Why don't we, instead, recognize the fact that we're observing a chink in the armor of maturity—and through that chink peers a wide-eyed little boy silently pleading for special attention, yes, for "mothering." Rather than administering a bitter dose of sarcasm, wife, when your husband becomes a little boy because he's sick, *baby him!*

And do it out of a genuinely loving, gently smiling heart.

Part of a wife's impatience with her husband's boyishness comes because she over-looks her own girlishness. There is a good deal of little girl still playing hide-and-seek inside each of us, no matter what our age. Why else do we get a mad urge to make a snow angel? Why do we long for roses instead of toasters, or candy rather than towels, as gifts?

Yet another aspect of maleness that bedevils many a wife is its relative inflexibil-ity. It usually doesn't take a woman long to notice the fact that once made "whole" by marriage, a man pretty much follows a straightforward, single-minded course through life. He seems seldom to look either right or left. In the meantime, his wife is con-stantly adjusting to accommodate him.

Probably while still on the honeymoon each mate discovers in the other traits and habits hitherto unrevealed. Men pretty well take those realities in stride. Women tend to stumble, to halt, bewildered and hurt, over pebbles in the pathway of true love.

One laughable "pebble" is the matter of learning to sleep together. Both newlyweds are accustomed to sleeping alone. That single-sleeper habit is deeply ingrained—approximately twenty years' worth. Suddenly, upon marriage, the familiar single bed gives place to a double bed—a bed with another body in it! There are, of course, pleasures in the adjustment, but there can also be some minor traumas. Chances are your husband adjusts quickly and well. He continues to sleep spread-eagle in the middle of the bed, just as he has all those years of his singleness. Even a medium-sized male spread-eagled in a double bed leaves precious little room for the bride. Flexibility comes into play. Common sense tells her there is no room in that bed for her own (former) spread-eagle sleep position. So she adjusts. She learns to curl, kittenlike, in the upper corner of what is theoretically her side of the bed.

Should this contrast in degrees of flexibility make us wives feel combative or martyred? No. I have heard it said that part of the original meaning in the Hebrew words for "help meet" is the idea of a woman's *adaptation* to her husband. So, you see, this differentiation is a long-standing one indeed!

Not all the adjustments must be or should be made by the wife. The man who demands that extreme is entirely off base spiritually, logically, and practically. As a man "dwells with his wife according to knowledge," he, too, will make adjustments for the sake of harmony. Yet the fact remains that in most cases it's the she, not the he, who must exercise the greater flexibility. I believe this relationship is implied in Ephesians 5:23-24,

> *Adaptation is an integral part of submission.*

where we're told, "For the husband is the head of the wife, even as Christ is the head of the church: and he is the saviour of the body. Therefore as the church is subject unto Christ, so let the wives be to their own husbands in every thing." Adaptation is an integral part of submission. Extending the body-and-head illustration used in Scripture, think about the relative observable adaptation of each. Clearly, it is the body that does the greater part.

Still, some wives are inwardly saying, "It's not fair! He seems to be excused for his shortcomings because he's a man; I'm supposed to eliminate my imperfect reactions!?" The man is *not* excused. He is individually accountable to God. Because of the emphasis

23

the Lord puts upon marriage and the picturing of Christ by the husband, the burden of responsibility on his shoulders is a heavy one. *Both* husband and wife in every marriage need a good deal of reworking. But we women somehow have an element within us that wants to do our own husband reconstruction. A wife's efforts to change her husband can be likened to trying to remove freckles with an ice pick. She helps nothing; she only hurts very deeply. Husband restructuring must be turned over to the one who made your man in the first place. Only He can reach the soul and spirit in which his flaws originate. In the process of turning the matter over to God, a wife usually finds that the divine hand begins reworking *her*, as well as her husband.

One of the joys of traveling and meeting large numbers of people is the opportunity to observe many Christian marriages. The most successful of those marriages are ones in which the wife has cheerfully adapted to her husband. Yes, even (or perhaps outstandingly!) in cases in which the need for adaptation has been obvious. When the "prickliness" of the husband's personality, pursuits, and/or performance would be enough to drive many a woman loony. Let me list a few examples:

❦ The man who didn't marry until well into mid-life and who maintained all of his bachelor idiosyncrasies.

❦ The husband who militaristically ordered domestic affairs—choosing his wife's and children's clothing, setting a daily housekeeping/cooking schedule, and checking up on every detail therein.

❦ The "super-drive" executive who constantly made business and social arrangements entailing hours of adjustment, house rearrangement, and cooking for his wife—many of them the last-minute variety.

❦ The man whose required business travel was extended by a poorly disguised preference for travel over domesticity.

❦ The man whose personal likes and dislikes invariably dictated meals, vacations, and house decor.

❦ The husband who was consumed with hunting trips to such a degree that the bulk of his paycheck went to support his hobby, while his wife's wardrobe and kitchen necessities were put on hold.

Ribbing Him Rightly

Those are only a very few of the hard-to-live-with men who come immediately to mind. I wish I could personally place a laurel wreath on the brow of each wife. Those ladies have done a superlative job of adapting. They have wisely resisted trying to change their men. They have not been retaliatory. Rather, they have allowed pressure to mold them into shining examples of Christian womanhood.

Human masculinity: definite, different, and demanding *flexibility* of the wife. So there it is, wife. Your life, responsibility, and joy are all bound up in your non-fairy-tale *man*.

Chapter Three

Exclusive Ribs, Inc.

Wouldn't it be wonderful if this wifing business could be reduced to a clear, paint-by-number pattern? But it doesn't— and indeed can't—work that way. One of the main reasons is the individuality of husbands. In basic physical form men are alike; there the likeness ends. One of the awesome marvels of God's creation is His infinite number of variations upon the basic human theme. As with snowflakes, so with people: no two are alike. That, of course, contributes incalculably to life's interest—and its problems!

Ribbing Him Rightly

Your husband is unlike any other in the world. He is a one-of-a-kind specimen. The only way to rib the guy properly and adequately is to *know* him, which in turn means, really, a lifelong study.

So then, wives, let's tackle the task of Husband Study. We'll begin with the obvious: physique. Right now, without him in sight, *describe him physically*. Give a precise, detailed description. "Brown hair, hazel eyes" won't do. What *shade* of brown is his hair? Are its highlights gold or red? Does he have gray in his hair, and where? Where on his head does his hair swirl in its growth? Where is his hairline on forehead, temples, and neck? Now you get an idea of how very detailed this Husband Study should be. And this is only the first item of the first section of the study! Go on in that intensive detailing through the following:

EYES
1. Color _____
2. Shape _____
3. Lashes and brows _____
4. Distinguishing characteristics _____

_____

FACE
5. Shape _____

6. Distinguishing characteristics _____

_____

NOSE
7. Shape/size _____

8. Distinguishing characteristics _____

_____

MOUTH
9. Size in proportion to face _____

10. Shape of lips _____

11. Unconscious expression _____

12. Distinguishing characteristics _____

_____

TEETH
13. Alignment _____

14. Color _____

15. Distinguishing characteristics _____

_____

CHIN
16. Shape _____

17. Distinguishing marks _____

_____

NECK
18. Long? Short? Average? _____

19. Collar size _____

SHOULDERS
20. Shape/breadth _____
21. Posture _____

TRUNK
22. Suit size _____
23. Long/short waisted? _____
24. Weight distribution _____
25. Distinguishing characteristics _____
_____

ARMS
26. Sleeve length _____
27. Muscular development _____

HANDS
28. Glove size _____
29. Length/shape of fingers _____

LEGS
30. Inseam length _____
31. Distinguishing characteristics _____
_____

FEET
32. Shoe size _____
33. Distinguishing characteristics _____
_____

In attempting to fill in the blanks, have you been embarrassed by your vague grasp of such details? If so, face up to your

carelessness and begin replacing it with concentration.

A study of his preferences should
come next.

ABOUT HIMSELF

34. What does he feel is his best character
quality? _____

35. How would he classify his personality? __

_____

36. What does he consider his best physical
feature? _____

37. What physical feature would he like to
change if possible? _____

38. What is his usual workday dress? _____

39. What would he choose to wear if he
could? _____

40. What does he consider his best color? __

_____

41. Does he like to have you choose or help
choose his clothing? _____

42. How does he feel about his leadership
ability? _____

ABOUT YOU

43. What does he like you to weigh? _____

44. What hairstyle does he prefer on you?

_____

45. Which of your casual outfits is his favorite? _____

46. Which dressy outfit? _____

47. Which nightgown? _____

48. What does he consider your best color?

_____

49. Is he pleased with your grooming? _____

_____

ABOUT YOUR HOUSE

50. What is his favorite household task?

_____

51. What is his UNfavorite job? _____

52. Which room does he feel most comfortable in? _____

53. Does he feel good about coming home at night? _____

54. Does he take interest/pride in your house? _____

55. What colors does he like used in decorating? _____

56. What colors does he *dislike* in decor?

_____

57. How does he rate your housekeeping?

_____

ABOUT FOOD

58. What is his favorite meal of the day?

_____

59. What is his least favorite dish?

_____

60. How does he like his eggs cooked?

_____

61. What dessert does he find most tempting?

_____

62. Does he appreciate exotic foods? _____
63. What is his least favorite way of serving his favorite meat? _____

ABOUT THE CHILDREN

64. At what age(s) did he feel most comfortable with the children? _____

      (Some men are scared to handle a baby because it's "fragile," but they love the grade-school, rough-and-tumble age.)

65. Does he prefer being with the children as a group or in a one-on-one setting? _____
66. Is he pleased with the children's character development? _____
67. Does he relate better to his son(s) or his daughter(s)? _____

ABOUT YOUR SOCIAL LIFE

68. Does he like the same people you like?

_____

69. Does he enjoy social occasions? _____

70. Do people react more positively to one of you than to the other? _____

It will also be beneficial to do some in-depth thinking about your husband's background. He is today what he began to be yesterday.

FAMILY

71. What was the social level of his family?

_____

72. What was the geographical orientation of his childhood? _____

73. Did his mother and father have a happy marriage? _____

74. If there was a divorce or death, how old was he when it occurred? _____

75. To which parent did he relate more strongly? _____

76. Did his father exert strong home leadership? _____

77. How many sisters and brothers did he have? _____

78. Was his disciplinary upbringing strict or lax? _____

79. Was his childhood marred by parental neglect, unfairness, or mistreatment? _____

80. If so, what was the nature of it? _____

_____

81. What is his adult attitude toward it?

_____

82. Was love openly expressed in his home?

_____

83. Is there presently a good relationship with his parents? _____

EDUCATION

84. What level of formal education did he complete? high school, college, advanced degree, technical training? _____

85. Were his grades low, average, high? _____

86. Were his scholastic experiences basically positive? _____

87. How successfully did he relate to fellow students? _____

88. Was he active in sports? Which one(s)?

_____

89. Was he primarily a leader or a follower in school? _____

90. Who was his favorite teacher? Why?

_____

91. How does he feel now about his educational preparation? _____

JOB

92. Does he feel adequately prepared for the job he holds? _____

93. Is it the thing he wanted to do as he looked forward to maturity? _____

94. Does he enjoy his work? _____

95. Does he find challenge in it? _____
96. Has he won the advancement he thinks he should have? _____
97. Does he prefer the people or the procedure of his job? _____
98. Does he feel threatened by some circumstance or person connected with his job?

These listings are by no means exhaustive. But they can give you an idea about the intensity of study you can—and should—do of that fellow you're wifing. Be sure you don't answer anything according to what you *think* you know about him! There are probably few wives who, at one time or another, have not been jolted by realizing they'd been making a wrong assumption about their husband. I have.

My jolt came during a casual social evening. Several couples were having a snacks-and-games get-together at the home of a friend. One of the games played was The Newlyweds Game. For those of you who don't recognize it, the basic purpose in the game is to test the knowledge of mates about each other. During one session of play, Bob was asked a series of questions about his preferences while I was kept in another room out of hearing distance. Then I was brought in, asked the same questions, and challenged to respond with the answers I thought he would have given. I bit the dust on the subject of eggs. When asked, "What is his favorite way to have eggs cooked," I confidently replied, "Scrambled," but I was dumbfounded to learn that Bob had answered, "Fried." I had been scrambling our breakfast eggs faithfully for years, *assuming* I knew my husband's prefer-ence; after all, it was mine! On the way home from the party, I asked Bob why he had never told me he preferred fried eggs. He gave the classic male response: "You never asked me." The point is, ladies, we need to ask our men these things so that we have a true picture of their individuality.

> *A wife's study of her husband should not be a one-time thing.*

Actually, a wife's study of her hus-band's unique self should not be just a one-time thing. It should last throughout their years together. Harking back to our per-sonal experience, I could compound the mis-take by thinking Bob will always prefer fried eggs long after his tastes have changed. Life is a process of changing. Those changes affect

men just as they do women. If a woman care-
lessly loses track of her man's true self to any
degree, she fails to the same degree to be a
wife whose perception consistently builds up
her marriage.

The study of a husband's individuality
is only the beginning. Even the most intensive study proves worthless if the findings are
not correctly used.

With completed study firmly in mind,
we may proceed to the next step. All that concentration is not for the purpose of protesting
about your husband's peculiarities. Nor will it
do any good to sit wishing he were otherwise
than he is. The right kind of response is actually a spiritual exercise made up of four parts:
acknowledgement, acceptance, attention, and
admiration.

Acknowledgement. This means seeing your husband as a unique creation of God.
Digest the thoughts of Psalm 139:14-16 as
they apply to your man.

I will praise thee; for I am fearfully
and wonderfully made: marvellous are thy
works; and that my soul knoweth right
well. My substance was not hid from thee,
when I was made in secret, and curiously
wrought in the lowest parts of the earth.

Thine eyes did see my substance, yet being unperfect [unformed]; and in thy book all my members were written, which in continuance were fashioned, when as yet there was none of them.

In other words, a man is not just the result of a biological process, a random combination of genetic factors. He, like you, is a specifically designed human being, a one-and-only specimen as personally formed by the mind of God as was Adam. Our Creator God can say to each of us, as He said to Jeremiah, "Before I formed thee in the belly I knew thee" (Jeremiah 1:5a). The concept of that unique creation can give a woman a whole new outlook on her man—this man to whom she is wife.

Acceptance. This means taking your husband as he is. This is not just a matter of will power or positive thinking. Genuine acceptance is a transaction between a woman and God: a transaction in which she says, in essence, "Lord, I recognize the fact that my husband is Your creation, that he has been made according to the plan of Your wisdom. I acknowledge Your wisdom to be as far above mine as the heavens are above the earth; therefore, Your creation of my husband makes

it unnecessary and wrong for me to try to re-
make him in any way. I accept him just as he
is, and I do so with gratitude."

Attention. Throughout her married
life a woman should keep her man the human
center of her attention. It is dangerously easy
to let him get partially or wholly hidden by
other demands of life such as the children,
the house and its upkeep, and a job. The most
common shift of attention occurs when children come into the home. Maternal instinct
begins operating on all eight cylinders, and
concentration roars off along the road of
motherhood, leaving a husband in the dust.
To let that happen is to invite domestic disaster. It is essential that a woman remember
God's pronouncement that "they [two] shall be
one flesh." Not three, four, or five! Children
leave; only husband and wife cleave! Too
many Christian women reverse those words
"leave" and "cleave" and their underlying principle. As a result, we see broken homes all
around us.

Admiration. In speech and in action,
we should communicate to our husbands the
fact that we admire them. In human terms,
every wife should have a hero—her own husband. This admiration must, of course, be

genuine. The wife who praises her husband verbally while criticizing him mentally is a hypocrite, and her basic insincerity is sensed by the husband.

Is wifely admiration scripturally supportable? Yes. Read the Song of Solomon. Throughout the book, the wife is lavish in her verbal admiration of her husband.

His response is typically masculine and universally instructive. He thrives in the glow of admiration, and he responds to her with adoration.

A negative illustration from Scripture is also timely. Go to the book of Proverbs and notice the number of times the "strange woman," or harlot, uses flattery to lure her victims. Obviously, man responds to admiration. The wife who withholds it increases her husband's vulnerability to extramarital attractions. Men who break their marriage vows often do so with women who are not as physically attractive as their wives. The straying husband may explain, "She makes me feel good about myself!" Admiration. It's a potent, important ingredient in wise wifing.

Your husband is a wonderfully unique creation of God's hand. He is unlike my husband—or anyone else's. God has entrusted

Ribbing Him Rightly

him to you that you might know him in the
most profound sense of the word, and that by
knowing, you might become the uniquely
suited, exclusively adapted helpmeet he needs.

$\wp$

Chapter Four

Of Ribs and Ears

Bone marrow serves as a factory producing both red and white blood cells, and those new cells number into the millions upon millions each day. Just as blood cells are essential to the human body, so too the element of communication is essential to marriage.

Without good *communication*, two people living in the same house can be virtual strangers to one another. It is as if they are moving along through life on two separate, nonconverging tracks. Marriage, however, is not meant to be parallelism, but unity.

Ribbing Him Rightly

What about our communication skills? Women characteristically have greater linguistic and expressive ability than men. It arises from that basic brain-hemisphere orientation mentioned earlier. But expression is not the whole of communication.

Real communication is like a tennis game. The ball of expression goes back and forth between the two players, and the manner in which either player sends the ball toward the other is crucial. So, wives, let's first of all consider a few principles of effective oral expression as they apply specifically to marriage.

First, *keep your emotions in check* when talking to your husband. Feminine emotionalism is disconcerting to a man. Not only does it make him feel uncomfortable; but it also can make his strongly logical mind assume that his wife's reasoning abilities have taken flight, thereby nullifying both the importance and the accuracy of what she is saying. Also, which of us would deny that, under the pressure of emotionalism, we usually say exactly what we shouldn't and forget to say what we should?

One thing that is helpful in avoiding emotionalism is to talk things out before they become unmanageably large. The woman who "keeps things to herself because she doesn't want to upset her husband" is actually doing him more cruelty than kindness. When she finally does get around to talking, her erupting feelings can splatter the subject, herself, and her husband all over the ceiling!

Second, *choose your talking times wisely.* The end of your husband's workday, before he has had a chance to eat, takes the prize as one of the *worst* times for meaningful discussions. A wife's recitation of domestic woes the moment he comes in the door ultimately can make him wish he didn't have to come home.

Third, *control your tone.* Have you ever listened to your own voice when you're trying to get a point across to your husband? Try it. You may be shocked to hear one or more of the following: whining, harshness, coldness, and/or accusation. The tone of voice in which we speak influences the way a listener receives and reacts to a message. Words that sound like bullets make a fellow want to hide—not heed.

> *The tone of voice influences the way a listener receives and reacts to a message.*

Fourth, *check your motivation and your spirit.* A message addressed to your husband for the sake of one-upmanship, self-gratification, or instruction is better left undelivered. Communication that is reactionary and fueled by vindictiveness should remain in the Dead Letter Department. In spite of attempts to camouflage your spirit, it will make itself known to your mate. Even more important, it is already known to God.

In those times of communication that honesty terms arguments, all of the preceding principles apply, and some extra restraints are also needed. First, fight clean. Battle the problem—don't butcher the person! Second, use "I" more than "you" in your speech. "I felt hurt . . ." or "I understood you to mean . . ." are far wiser and more effective than "you were cruel . . ." or "you said. . . ." The "you" approach is accusatory. It is like a battering ram, and your mate's reaction to it, quite naturally, will be self-protection, retaliation, or avoidance.

Speaking is only one half of communication. The other half is listening. A great many women fail badly in the latter. Some years ago, while studying for a lecture on etiquette, I read a statement in some now-forgotten source: "The good listener not only is welcome in any conversation; he also *learns*

something." There is no area of life where
that principle is more strategic than in the
marital relationship.

The well-greased jaw is a troublesome
human trait, as clearly indicated by both the
Old and New Testaments. It also rates lowest
with regard to perception. We don't come to
understand another person by talking to him
but by listening to him.

So let's concentrate for a moment or
two on the characteristics of good listening.

First, *give your attention to the speaker.*
That seems self-evident, doesn't it? But think
back to the past twenty-four hours and the
times therein when you've done something
else while your husband talked to you. Maybe
it was washing the dinner dishes, or anything,
no matter how legitimate, that took your attention off your husband and what he was
saying. After all, how do you like talking to
someone who only half listens? He feels the
same way. You can discourage and kill a husband's verbal sharing by allowing your attention to be diverted.

Second, *listen with your eyes as well as
your ears.* Eyes are our primary interpersonal
members, our means of contacting the real
self. Where do you look while your husband

talks to you? Past his left shoulder? At the chandelier? Out the window? At the floor? Eliminate those improper focus points— fast—and look at the speaker! Consider how basic that principle is to being a good audience member for a public speaker. We know it's rude to avoid looking at him, don't we? It's also rude when "only" he is speaking. And foolish! Much of communication is visual rather than verbal: facial expressions, nervous mannerisms, body positions, and gestures. Those things help us know what the other person is really saying. If we're not using our eyes, we miss important clues.

Third, *listen with interest*. I know, some of the things he likes to talk about are not "right up your alley" of interest. Airplanes, sports, or capital gains may not increase your heart rate at all. Nor do you necessarily need to like them. After all, a man enjoys having a bit of exclusive expertise! But we wives do need, always, to be interested in his interest!

Fourth, *ask good questions*. Questions demonstrate interest and encourage your man to continue and expand his communication. Be sure that the questions you ask aren't challenging or critical. Some wives seem to delight in what might be called a "Pearl Harbor complex"—they dive-bomb every little ship of thought their husbands try to float! If that doesn't start a marital world war, it will drive the victim deep into the hills of silence.

Fifth, *don't be thinking of what you want to contribute* to the conversation while he's talking. That kills both attention and understanding. You may come up with a terrific $2 response, but you may pay for it with a $10 debit on his desire to share his thoughts with you.

Sixth, *don't be too quick to respond.* Rapid-fire return tells your husband two things: you haven't considered his words with much thought, and you'd rather talk than listen. Consider what God says in the Book of Proverbs: "He that answereth a matter before he heareth it, it is folly and shame unto him" (18:13). And James reminds us, "Let every man be swift to hear, slow to speak, slow to wrath" (1:19).

At this point, experience tells me there are some of you asking, "But what if my husband *won't talk to me*?" The unfunny cartoon of the man in front of the TV set, unfortunately, identifies much of husbanddom.

Your husband simply may be the non-verbal type. Unless you were exceedingly unbright, you perceived that fact before marriage. Why should matrimony change his basic nature? Your part is to adjust to his quietness, while always maintaining a warm, receptive spirit that encourages him to talk if and when the inclination should strike him. Also, don't feel that you are obligated to fill the silences. There can be sweet, happy communion in *quietness* you know!

It is also possible that your husband's retreat into silence is just that. A retreat—from you. You unwittingly may have brought about that retreat by one or more of the following:

- Out-talking him. At last, he gets weary of struggling against the ever-flowing current of words. He chooses to float on the relatively serene pond of silence.

- "Listening" with impatience.

- A critical attitude (expressed as clearly facially as verbally) toward what he has said or tried to say. He shields himself in silence's armor.

- A scornful attitude. "How could you think/do/say such a thing" can choke off a fellow's communication posthaste.

☘ A battle for headship in the home, either spoken or implied. For the sake of peace, a man may take shelter behind the wall of silence.

☘ Badgering him to talk. The more you urge, the less inclined he feels to cooperate.

"Well!" some feisty wife may snort. "Why doesn't my husband stand up and fight like a man? Why would he run and hide? Is he a mute?" The answer is multifaceted, I think. In the first place, the wounds given by a wife are the most painful and deeply scarring he can know in his adult life. Also, a man's delicate sense of self *cannot* take endless battering from the one who should be his best ally. He must flee in self-preservation. Finally, fighting runs counter to his innate protectiveness toward the female of the species.

> *From a wife who knows how to listen flow the health-building "corpuscles" of heart contact.*

Let's move on now to contemplate some of the "red corpuscles" that good listening injects into the bloodstream of a marriage.

Ribbing Him Rightly

From a wife who knows how to listen
flow the health-building "corpuscles" of heart
contact. The Bible reminds us that "out of the
abundance of the heart the mouth speaketh"
(Matthew 12:34). Wives who listen consistently and carefully have, as it were, a finger
on their husband's pulse. Months and years of
listening will teach a wife not only *what* her
husband thinks but also *how* he thinks. She'll
know, in other words, something of the state
of his heart—that heart from which spring all
of his thoughts, actions, and attitudes.

Far too many Christian wives have
foolishly neglected the function of listening.
They have opted to place their attention on
the talk of TV, children, or someone outside
the home, feeling that their husband's exterior
was enough for their attention, that the inter-
nal man "was then, is now, and ever shall be"
the same. Those women now sit bewailing
broken homes. Immediately to mind comes a
wife who *didn't listen* when her husband said he
didn't want to have children, who *didn't listen*
when he said he was tired of take-out and
frozen foods, who *didn't listen* when he sug-
gested she stay more in the home and less at
the office. Who *didn't listen*—period. Her be-
lated wail, "I never dreamed he would turn to

another woman . . . ," echoes still through the ruins of her marriage.

The listening wife also injects corpuscles called "talk therapy" into her marriage. Men (just like women) need to talk, to keep someone up-to-date on their accomplishments, and to have someone see and share the dreams, hopes, doubts, and fears they keep locked away from everyone else. No, in the strictest sense she can't *do* anything in those areas, yet she does much by providing an outlet for the inner man, who is otherwise isolated and mouldering behind the strong iron bars of nonexpression.

Finally, the wife who recognizes and exercises her auditory role provides a disease-fighting mechanism by remaining *aware*. The importance of staying up-to-date with each other, your different worlds, and your relationship can't be too strongly stressed. Into the incision between today and yesterday—or last month or last year—or whenever you last really listened to your husband, Satan can drop some mighty deadly germs!

For the believer, vertical communication must shape, restrain, and direct horizontal communication. Therefore, the real key to right communication in a Christian marriage is to talk more to God about your mate than you talk to your mate . . . and to listen care-fully—and obediently—as God talks to you through His Word.

❧

Chapter Five

Rock-Ribbed Support

A rib is bone. Bone: the hard material in the body that makes up its structurally necessary framework.

Supportiveness is undeniably one of the most important purposes a wife can fulfill. In courtship and newlywed days, being "little Miss/Mrs. Admiration" is lots of fun. But somewhere along the road of marriage, the glow tends to fade from the face, the sparkle from the eyes, and the smile from the lips of the wife beholding her husband.

The fade-out begins when the Mrs. recognizes that her Mr. is not a combination

of Harold Handsome, Bradley Brilliant,
Melvin Muscle, and George Generous. Mr.
Handsome may have a wart under his left ear,
Sir Brilliant makes incredibly dumb state-
ments, Mr. Muscle may be afraid of heights,
and Sir Generous may decide to buy a tractor
rather than a new dining room suite. Oops!
Where's all the shiny-eyed admiration *then*?

Actually, admiration for Handsome-
Generous is part of infatuation's froth because the creature admired simply does not
exist. The sooner a wife settles that fact in her
mind, the better off she, her husband, and
their marriage will be. It might help to say it
in unison, ladies: *There is no perfection this side
of heaven.*

So then we're to support—consistently—this less-than-perfect fellow to whom
we (who are also less than perfect) have become attached by marriage? Absolutely.

If a man is to stand strong, whole, and
undamaged, he must have his wife's support.
Again, the physical function of ribs eloquently
presents the case for us, particularly as the
ribs are tied in to important muscles. In other
words, the ribs help make possible much of
the body's mobility and flexibility.

What is supportiveness, exactly? How does a wife best carry out this function? Ribs provide support as an integral part of the body itself. You and your husband share humanity. So ask yourself what *you* find supportive. Just a brief listing might include:

&Verbal encouragement

&Admiration for personal qualities

&Commendation for accomplish-

  ments

&Reassurance in disappointment

&Sympathy in failure

But does a *man* need those things? Just as surely, as critically, as a body needs ribs!

Verbal encouragement. A man may rarely, if ever, express self-doubt. But it's there, wife! Self-doubt can discomfit life's accomplishments, cripple confidence, and cause a hidden emotional consumption that is clumsily covered by over-aggressiveness. Unsure moments come to each of us. At such times, there's nothing like having solidity re-established by an encouraging word from someone beloved. His sense of self-worth is as essential to a man as the diaphragm, the chief muscle of breathing, is to the human body. And what anchors that essential muscle? The ribs.

Admiration for personal qualities.

No one needs to urge us to point out a man's flaws, does he? But we're incredibly slow to see and admire his strong points! The heart of a man cries out for support because he really doesn't like himself very much. Now this is a point at which some wives come to a mulish balk. They point to things like their husbands' braggadocio, the frequent flattering attention given him by others, and so on, as sure signs that their men do not need wifely admiration. But those objections focus on externals rather than the internals of their husbands. Outward preening can cover deep inward pain at the lack of the *one* support the fellow craves, his wife's. Admiration from other quarters may tickle his ears, but that of his nearest and dearest gives his *heart* the boost it needs.

Admiration of his nearest and dearest gives his heart the boost it needs.

Some women will protest, "I don't admire my husband. Am I supposed to lie?" No, you don't lie. You *look*. Look for something you do, or should, appreciate in him. Oddly enough, you are likely to find admirable qualities on the reverse side of the very things that irritate you. For example, stop glaring at his maddening stubbornness long enough to see the positive—his strength of will. I remember talking to a wife whose husband outsiders termed "bullheaded." She recognized the fact that he grated on people, but she called the trait "strong individuality." That wife is right on target! Dear lady, one of the most important love deeds you can perform for your husband (and for your children, as they look on) is recognition of and praise for his admirable qualities. And remember especially to admire his *masculine* qualities.

Commendation for accomplishments. Why wait until he makes a million-dollar deal? Commend him on the swing set he put together for the children, or the excellent Sunday school lesson he presented, or the tile he laid in the hall bathroom. "Accomplishments" needn't be spelled in all capital letters! Your husband *does* accomplish things every day, things that benefit you, the family, and others. A husband needs to have those for whom he's providing acknowledge his accomplishments. Lacking wifely commendation, his heart utters the sad sigh, "I guess I just don't do much that's worthwhile." Watch out for that unsupported muscle!

Reassurance in disappointment. Do you recognize the fact that your husband comes home perhaps daily, and certainly weekly, with disappointments weighing him down? It's not necessarily the size of the disappointments that brings discouragement and defeat but the accumulation. Wouldn't it seem natural that a wife would be sensitive to her husband's small defeats? But that's not the case. The noises of daily living can drown out the sound of his quiet sigh. Sometimes, too, a wife's attitude toward her husband's burdens is that of an uneasy resentment, resentment that he brings his troubles home when she already has more than she can handle with house, children, and self.

The chest muscles, rib-attached, make inhalation possible. A husband's spirit, wife-reassured, makes courageous persistence possible. Proverbs 18:14 certainly applies here: "The spirit of a man will sustain his infirmity; but a wounded spirit who can bear?"

Sympathy in failure. Invincible, he isn't. But he desperately wants to be. A man has a built-in desire to live as a hero before his own little flock. He wants the fruit of his labors to be rich and abundant. Yet because we live in a sin-cursed world, failure haunts his pathway. It can come early or late; it can come unexpectedly; it can come repeatedly. Whenever and however it strikes, failure knocks the wind and the heart out of a man. At such times, a wife's sympathy ministers to her husband. Her quiet "coming alongside him" soothes his pain and gives him strength to regroup his resources and re-enter the fray.

Supportiveness: a strategic function of ribs and wives. Yet there is sometimes a strange perversity in us women, a perversity that majors on removing supports rather than placing them! At just this juncture in my writing, I witnessed a classic case of prop-pulling.

Our family was vacationing with friends at a ski resort. One afternoon I chose to retire (maybe "retreat" would be the better word) early from the slopes. With skis, ski poles, and aching muscles, I stood in front of the lodge waiting for the shuttle vehicle, which would take me back to our quarters. All at once, from the main entrance of the ski lodge came a shrill female voice: "Don't you ever say that again!" A middle-aged woman from whom the shouting was coming clearly proclaimed anger by her posture, walk, and facial expression. Beside her, looking like a whipped dog, walked her husband. As far as I could tell, he never said a word in either self-defense or retaliation. It seemed apparent that the poor fellow had done something wrong in the preceding few minutes, and his wife was not about to help him survive or forget it. As they crossed the street she again yelled at him (he was walking right beside her!), "I've told you five or six times. . . ." Then, thankfully, the couple moved out of my hearing range.

Scenes similar to that one are played daily in homes of unsaved and saved alike— women reacting to their husbands' failures, disappointments, and mistakes in such a way that they add to the agony rather than alleviate it. I've done that—haven't you? The reason for such reprehensible behavior must lurk in the subterranean depths of fallen human nature: the "This proves I was right in what I've thought all along," delight in seeing "the bigger guy" take a fall, or primitive bloodlust. Who knows? Whatever the reason, it's a mighty ugly one. The bones have been snatched away from the stricken, quivering muscles.

Supportiveness is much more than lightly uttered words of cheer and reassurance. It should be an integral part of every wife's structure. She should give support because her character, placement, and function are marked by sturdiness.

Supportiveness is based upon belief. Whoever else may lose faith, you must believe in him. That kind of ribbing can virtually rescue and rebuild a man.

Note again the title of this chapter: "Rock-Ribbed Support." There may be times when it is extremely difficult for a wife to be supportive. It's pretty easy to speak words of encouragement when he's the only one who's down. But what happens in a situation in which the wife is battling the nausea of early pregnancy, one toddler has chicken pox, the other has an ear infection, the dog just produced a litter of thirteen—and THEN the husband loses his job? With every circumstance legislating against and her own emotions challenging the necessity, how does a woman dredge up encouragement for her husband? She first must enhance her own solidity. The principle here is that of rescue from quicksand. If both parties are trapped by the engulfing substance, there is no way one

> *Whoever else may lose faith, you must believe in him.*

can help the other. One of them must be upon solid ground! No flesh-and-blood female can, from her easily exhausted natural resources, reach a suppor-tive hand to her husband when she herself is sinking. She needs an unshakable foundation and supernatural strength. And for that kind of help she must flee to God's Word. It will provide iron-veined empowering like the following:

"As ye have therefore received Christ Jesus the Lord, so walk ye in him: Rooted and built up in him, and stablished in the faith, as ye have been taught, abounding therein with thanksgiving" (Colossians 2:6-7).

"I can do all things through Christ, which strengtheneth me" (Philippians 4:13).

"But my God shall supply all your need according to his riches in glory by Christ Jesus" (Philippians 4:19).

"Finally, my brethren, be strong in the Lord, and in the power of his might" (Ephesians 6:10).

As the strength of God's Word infuses her, the wife must also seek motivation from the Word to offer support to her husband.

Our human self-centeredness makes us willing to rest in the fulfillment of our own needs. We fear depletion of our supply by another's demand. But God gives that we may give in turn:

"Blessed be God, even the Father of our Lord Jesus Christ, the Father of mercies, and the God of all comfort; Who comforteth us in all our tribulation, that we may be able to comfort them which are in any trouble, by the comfort wherewith we ourselves are comforted of God" (II Corinthians 1:3-4).

"Being enriched in everything to all bountifulness" (II Corinthians 9:11*a*).

"Bear ye one another's burdens, and so fulfill the law of Christ" (Galatians 6:2).

"Walk worthy of the vocation wherewith ye are called, with all lowliness and meekness, with longsuffering, forbearing one another in love; endeavoring to keep the unity of the Spirit in the bond of peace" (Ephesians 4:1*b*-3).

"And be ye kind one to another, tenderhearted, forgiving one another, even as God for Christ's sake hath forgiven you" (Ephesians 4:32).

Look not every man on his own things, but every man also on the things of others (Philippians 2:4).

It is by thus drawing upon God's resources that the dedicated wife maintains the strength of her own spiritual construction and lends solidity to her husband through supportiveness.

Finally, let us consider one area in which problems about supportiveness rear their heads: the situation in which a husband's mental/emotional/spiritual "low" is a result of his own doing. Many times, for instance, his abrasive personality has caused someone to react against him; or he has followed an unwise decision to its end in failure; or the thing he tried and failed to accomplish was far beyond his capabilities in the first place. Does the wife then let him "stew in his own juice"? No, she doesn't. It would be utmost cruelty to let the fellow boil himself alive! The wife's focus in this type of situation must be on the *man himself,* not his deed, attitude, decision, or personality. Only the lowest, most bitter scum of an enemy kicks a man when he's down! Admittedly, some of the cases will be hurtful to you as well as to him, so the role of innocent victim isn't easy to play. Still, the focus of concern must be on the heart of the main actor, your husband. For some of you, the years may be filled with your husband's failures, and you're sorely tempted to stop being supportive because of sheer weariness.

But remember the "seventy-times-seven" principle of forgiveness Jesus taught? That most-important-of-all human relationships, marriage, makes critical demands on that principle.

All in all, then, this responsibility to be supportive is neither minor nor light. It demands a woman—a rib—who is firmed up daily by the calcium and iron of God's Word.

Chapter Six

Ribs—Cage for His Heart

The most important organ pro-
tected by ribs is the heart. The most important part of a husband given into his wife's
care is his heart. Speaking about that fact,
Proverbs 31:11 holds a strongly convicting
phrase: "The heart of her husband doth safely
trust in her."

In marriage a man does indeed entrust
much into his wife's hands:

- He trusts her to fulfill her God-given
  role as helpmeet.

- He trusts her to act and react out of love.

℮ He trusts her to value and wisely use the material resources he provides.

℮ He trusts her to hear and hide the confidences of his heart.

℮ He trusts to her the ministry of encouragement and support in his uncertainties and disappointments.

℮ He trusts her to trust him with the leadership of their home.

℮ He trusts her to bear and nurture his children, protecting and investing that heritage of the Lord for His glory.

℮ He trusts her to keep their home a testimony to those outside and inside by keeping it clean, neat, and comfortable.

℮ He trusts her to honor her vow of devotion to him alone of all men. In all these ways and many more, he trusts her to be *trustworthy*.

The trust a man invests in his wife is indescribably extensive, important, and vulnerable. Yet many of us wives live marriage by rote or by will power, forgetful of the treasure of trust we possess.

Each time I concentrate upon the im-
mense amount of trust God and my husband
have placed in me by allowing me to be a wife,
I'm awed and humbled. The position is a priv-
ileged one, yet my performance in the position
frequently fails to measure up.

Because you and I, as wives, hold our
husbands' hearts, we should always take great
care to protect their hearts. But just how is
that done?

First, we protect a husband's heart
from outside dangers. We surround him with
our belief in him. His wife is the one person a
man should be able to count on as being on
his team. This was mentioned in an earlier
chapter, but it bears expansion. As he walks
through the mean, tough world, a man is
often cruelly attacked. He may be ridiculed,
ignored, harassed, threatened, or slandered.
Those attacks are intended to reach and de-
stroy him. They can be successful, too, unless
a wife protects his heart. The strength of her
loving belief in him can make any attack from
outside bearable.

I had frequently seen and read examples of this wifely function, but there came a
moment in my own marriage when the reality
of my protective role hit full force. Bob and I

had experienced the heartbreak of a rebellious child. We had tearfully and prayerfully reacted to the crisis. Most of our Christian friends surrounded us with love, comfort, and prayer. But not all. In the midst of our agony, some attacked my husband. They accused, scorned, belittled, upbraided, and generally tore him to shreds verbally. In bed one night, as he held me in his arms and told me what had been said, I cried helplessly over the unjust cruelty he had suffered. But it was his ending statement to the narrative that pierced me: "Sweetheart, it's *all right*—as long as we have the Lord and each other."

My protective role in that crisis was not played out in words. I was utterly helpless to express what I felt. It was, instead, experienced—a drawing together of our beings against emotional batterings.

Although we know that crisis points have the power to drive couples apart or to weld them together, we seldom consider the part choice plays in the matter. The crisis itself really is not the determining factor in the emotional direction taken. We choose which direction to take. Again, a personal experience showed me this truth.

Three years after we were married, Bob and I rejoiced to learn that I was expecting a baby. The full-term pregnancy was smooth and happy. On January 14 our first-born son made his appearance in the world. His stay, however, was only two hours long, for God called him home. In the unutterable agony of the days, weeks, and months that followed, there was a strong compulsion to curl up in isolation, overcome by the grief of my baby-empty arms. My weeping inner self scorned the thought that my husband could comprehend, compensate for, or comfort my loss. I stood at an emotional crossroads. In one illuminating midnight moment, I knew the choice was mine. The crisis was not the deciding factor: I held the power of decision. How would I choose to *respond* to the crisis? Deciding for isolation would have been destructive. Deciding to cleave to my husband would—and did—add depth, breadth, and beauty to our marriage.

That principle holds true in whatever crisis we experience as wives. Will we choose to let the heat of crisis dry and shatter us or melt and mold us? The decision is ours. Drawing away destroys. Drawing together builds.

Protecting his heart. What of those times when someone comes to you with a criticism of your husband? This is most often the case for those of us married to preachers, but lay couples experience this situation as well. The wife composed of human materials will feel an urge to sock the critic in the nose.

> *A man should feel he can share the deepest things of his heart with his wife.*

Though nose flattening may vent feelings, it's not the recommended Christian reaction. Instead, a silent "emergency prayer" for patience can bring a calmly stated response that the complaint must be taken directly to your husband. After that, a kind but firm refusal to continue the conversation is in order. Tell your husband of the matter, but do so factually rather than emotionally. You thus prepare him without predisposing him to any particular reaction. Beyond the actual moment of the criticism, it's important that the wife not brood and let the incident discolor her attitude toward the critic. (Obviously, that is a job for the Holy Spirit's assistance!)

Second, a wife protects her husband's heart by treasuring its secret expressions. This

function is tied in with listening. A man
should feel he can share the deepest things of
his heart with his wife. As he trusts her with
those innermost secrets, she has the responsibility to be trustworthy. That's not always as
easy as it might sound. There are times when
the expressions of a husband's heart do not
make his wife's heart jump for joy: he con-
fesses to a troubling temptation; he reveals a
train of thought that, if followed to its con-
clusion, portends trauma for the family; he
expresses disapproval or dislike for some
member of her family. Whatever the revela-
tion, there are several parts to the heart-trust
transaction. First, no matter what your husband confides, recognize his expression as a
healthy thing. It is far better for him to "get
something off his chest" than to withhold and
thus inwardly enlarge it. Let him know you
appreciate his sharing. Second, realize that an
expression of his heart does not mandate a response from you. A listening ear may be all he
needs. Third, if he indicates a desire for your
verbal response, give it prudently. There are
some responses to avoid: (1) a too-glib reassurance, (2) denial of what he feels to be a
problem, (3) shock or flaring anger, (4) disapproval or reproach, or (5) an instant-pudding

sermonette. As any red-blooded wife will quickly recognize, the ability to deny such responses demands *great* self-control. The Bible calls it having "rule over the spirit." Such rule comes through combined prayer for the Holy Spirit's control and the practical habit of biting one's tongue! But remember, your husband is trusting you with confidential information —trusting you to hear it rightly. When he expresses his heart's secrets, he's also trusting you to react in love. *Love is kind!* You don't need to put a stamp of approval upon everything he shares with you. You do have the responsibility to bathe the moment in love's kindness.

You must also be trustworthy by guarding the confidentiality of what he has expressed. Most Christian wives don't intentionally betray their husbands' confidence. They do so in unguarded, unpremeditated moments such as in trying to "explain" a husband's actions to mother, father, sister, and so on, or in contributing an illustrative tidbit in a "strictly closed, intimate" conversation among "the girls." The fact nevertheless stands: she has betrayed his confidence.

Finally, a wife must honor her husband's trust by not using his confidence as a

weapon against him. His heart's expression
can become a weapon if she (a) chalks it up in
her mind as a mark against him, (b) files it
away mentally for future reference in argument
situations, or (c) reacts calmly on the surface
but secretly treasures its hurtfulness as an in-
strument for her self-martyrdom.

Ribs protect the heart from outside
dangers. It is important, too, that they themselves not threaten the safety and health of
the heart. An outside knife wound can be less
deadly than an inner puncture from a rib!

Unhealthy ribbing can suffocate a
heart. Imagine a rib cage contracting, shrink-
ing, and closing in upon the heart. The destructive end is obvious. That does happen in
the physical sense, in rare instances. Its occur-
rence in the marital sense is much more common. Such destructive shrinkage is known as
overpossessiveness or jealousy.

Each of us probably knows one or
more women whose wifing would more accurately be termed "smothering." For whatever
reason, the wife feels insecure and fearful in
her relationship to her husband. She wants
him *always* at her side. She imagines that his
introduction to, or conversation with, another
woman threatens her hold on him. She fears

that even a glance elsewhere means he is longing for someone else. She distrusts his every absence from her, questions his explanations, and checks up on his whereabouts and activities. Such a wife is a pitiful thing, but pity does not excuse the fact that she has become a threat rather than a protection. Nor can she rightly claim "love" as the basis for her jealousy. Genuine love casts out fear and sets the loved object free.

The intensely jealous wife needs to realize that her spirit of fearful distrust will, like acid, eat away at the fabric of her marriage. And, sadly, the more tightly she clutches her husband, the less sure is her hold upon him. A man, understandably, feels stifled by his wife's jealousy. Her unreasoning suspicions and accusations bear in upon him with crushing pressure. Not only does he become miserable and frustrated, but he may actually be driven to do what his wife most fears! A jealousy-crushed man can reach the point of desperation that reasons, "She is convinced that my interests lie elsewhere. Nothing I do or say shakes her suspicions. I can't take it any more . . . I'm going to give up and live up to her expectations!"

This warning against jealousy does not mean we can naively assume that because our husbands are Christians they will not be tempted by the siren voices with which Satan will fill their ears. Our men are surrounded by females who resemble man-eating tigers. But all the suspicion and watchfulness in the world can't ensure our husbands' moral safety. We are far wiser to concentrate on being attractive, pleasant, loving, attentive, and exciting wives as we daily commit our men into God's keeping. Jealousy is not protective; it is destructive.

The trust of his heart. Of his *heart*. From far back in the reaches of time, the heart of man has been designated as the source of his emotions. It is a man's heart that first reaches out, tentatively, seeking the return of affection from that woman whose face, form, character, and personality attract him. If affection meets with affection, the heart's emotion solidifies and strengthens. Ultimately, the heart declares and commits itself. In the midst of candlelight and flowers, friends and family, two young people pledge themselves one to the other. The vows issue from the heart.

Ribbing Him Rightly

The lovely words of the wedding ceremony take but a moment. The living reality of the commitment demands a lifetime. Yet throughout the years, whether they be filled with laughter or weeping, hard times or pleasant, at the core of a marriage stand the hearts of man and wife. It is upon heart expression that the strength of a marriage depends. In closing this chapter, let's consider together the words, the works, and the worlds of the heart.

The words of the heart. The loving heart yearns to speak its love. Yet somehow, accumulating days and duties have a way of curtailing love's spoken word. In the busyness of living, "I love you" begins to seem almost extraneous. But we must never let those words remain unspoken. They are precious words that comfort, assure, and caress. If they are squeezed out of our lives, we, our husbands, our children, and our homes become paupers.

Perhaps the speaking of love is difficult for you because of the example your parents set. Some parents not only withhold verbal expression of love, but they consider the emotion itself a weakness. If you did not hear love's voice as a child, it seems foreign as an adult. But the learning of love's language

and ever-increasing fluency in it should be
the desire of every Christian wife.

The best way to learn to say "I love
you" is to say it. And keep saying it until you
not only feel comfortable with the words but
until you feel uncomfortable without them!
Nor do you wait for your husband's lead in
love's verbal expression. *Many men have a no-
toriously difficult time expressing emotion.* Your
warm, frequent verbalizing of love can help
free him from the bonds of awkwardness. Nor
should you wait for a certain setting in which
to voice those all-important words. Life is not
like television, with its soft romantic music
playing. More than likely, it's filled instead
with sounds of traffic, vacuum cleaners, children, and dogs. The words of love provide
music for the heart no matter what sounds fill
the ear. Feeling should likewise be ignored as
a prerequisite for speaking love. Feeling fluc-
tuates wildly. Love is an
abiding commitment of
the will. Those women
who demand the feel-
ing of love before they
will express love are
opting for comparative muteness. The bubbles
of the feelings of infatuation disintegrate

> *The words of love
> provide music for
> the heart.*

under the harshness of detergents and floor wax. No matter what your training, no matter what the setting or feeling, give voice to the love of your heart. His heart longs to hear you speak of your love.

The works of the heart. Love gives. God, who is Himself love, demonstrates that truth in the giving of His Son, Jesus Christ, to be our Savior. He in turn says to us, His born-again children, "If ye love me, do. . . ." The identical principle applies between husband and wife. She who loves—who rightly cares for the heart of her mate—not only speaks but also demonstrates her love. Throughout this book I've pointed out various aspects, or demonstrations of, wifely love. Now we'll look at just two more: caring for him and caring for herself.

Love declares itself in what it does, in how it cares for the loved one. The woman who has no interest in keeping her man's home clean, tidy, and comfortable has a love that is lacking. The wife who lets her husband go out of the house day after day with shirts unironed and suits unpressed is deficient in her love. The woman who begrudges cooking and slaps meals on the table any old way has a problem rooted in an anemic love. Some few

women reading this book will protestingly
point to an "exception status" for their marriage. "I married the wrong man," or "I married out of rebellion to my parents and to
God," or "This man has broken my heart!"
Those situations *do not* constitute exemptions.
The "wrong man" at the wedding is the "right
man" now that you're married. Rebellion-
prompted nuptials make scriptural obedience
even more important. Disappointment and
heartbreak given by one doesn't justify retaliation or retreat by the other. The biblical principle is *longsuffering* and *Spirit-empowered love*.
In such cases and others, when a woman has
reached the point of saying, "I don't love my
husband anymore," she can, with God's help,
rebuild that love. Just as she tore it down with
her own hands (Proverbs 14:1), she can rebuild it by *doing* the things that say "I care"
until, eventually, feeling is kindled or rekin-
dled.

The Lord has allowed me a tiny but illustrative experience of love's actions building
love's feelings. When our children were young,
our Stephen saved his money and cajoled his
daddy until he succeeded in acquiring a pet
guinea pig. I hadn't wanted the critter. I'd
protested the very thought of a smelly mem-

ber of the rodent family becoming a member
of ours. Nevertheless, Ziegfreid took up resi-
dence. I found absolutely nothing attractive in
his brown-and-white, tailless self. I was convinced that the whole situation was burden-
some and unfair! As the school year
progressed and Stephen got increasingly busy,
the daily care of Z. Jones fell my lot more and
more. I didn't like the animal, but I fed and
watered him simply out of humane responsibility. I hated his stinky cage, but I cleaned it
to avoid air pollution and nasal offense. Thus
the weeks and months passed as Stephen and
I took care of his pet. To my surprise, the
physical care given to Ziegfreid resulted in
emotional caring. Stephen found Ziggy dead
in his cage one morning. As my son and I
buried the little brown-and-white body, my
tears wet the grave along with Stephen's.

Love cares for—takes care of—the
one it loves. The works of love are the heart's
sign language, a language easily read by another heart.

The outstanding biblical instruction to
men is to love their wives. It follows, then,
that one way to demonstrate our caring for
our husbands is to be lovable. But what makes
a woman lovable? Needing the masculine

viewpoint, I asked my husband. The list he gave me is short but potent:

Number 1: Unpredictability. Surprised at that one? So was I. Bob explained, "Your unpredictability frustrates me sometimes, but it keeps you from ever seeming dull." No husband wants to be *bored* by his wife. It seems, then, that the old saying "Variety is the spice of life" applies in the life and love of marriage. Yet a word of caution is appropriate here. Unpredictability's spice must not be overpowering. Too much spice is as bad as too little.

Number 2: Softness. A man wants his wife to be *feminine*. Did you hear about the young fellow who went to a computer dating service? The consultant asked, "What are you looking for in a prospective wife?" The client replied, "Something warm, soft, and sweet." Fed that information, the computer buzzed, clicked, and whirred—then matched up the young man with a loaf of zucchini bread! That joke makes an interesting comment on how rare femininity is today. Among Christian women, however, femininity should be a universal characteristic.

Number 3: Vulnerability. A man wants to feel *needed*. To know that his wife feels incomplete without him, that she is not self-sufficient. Beware of becoming independent in your capabilities. If you are a whiz at minor house repairs, yard work, car care, bookkeeping, and so on, your husband can rightly begin to feel unneeded! The same danger lurks in a wife's sense of independence through working outside the home. "My paycheck" and "your paycheck" can bankrupt the unity of marriage. Because a man needs to be needed, his wife's self-sufficiency can drive him to seek a woman who makes him feel necessary.

Number 4: Excitability. Hebrews 13:4 says, "Marriage is honourable in all, and the bed undefiled." In the great majority of cases, clinical discussion of the physical relationship in marriage is unnecessary. For a woman, the keys to optimum excitability are *attitude* and *attention.*

A Christian woman with the attitude "The bedroom is the uncouth, distasteful part of marriage" is not the spiritual giant she may claim to be. How dare God's woman consider God's creation disgusting? The physical love between husband and wife is high and holy. Excitability. Is that really indicated by the Bible? Definitely. For instance, it can be

found in a small, generally unnoticed word—
a preposition—in Proverbs 5:18: "Rejoice
with the wife of thy youth." "With." Physical
union is meant to have a mystical, magical
beauty that touches both man and woman,
lifting them to the ecstatic heights of emotional experience. If your attitude runs in the
vein of "shameful, dirty, a chore," ask God to
help you replace those negatives with "right,
good, pure, spiritual, freeing, exalting." That
basic attitude change is a must for the
God-honoring woman.

Attention. A wife needs to focus upon
the moment and act of physical love.
Thoughts of tomorrow's menu, what Suzy said
about her teacher, the missing word for the
crossword puzzle, and so on—*all* need to be
banished. Mental distraction causes emotional distancing. Moreover, each one of us
Christian wives should develop bedroom al-
lure.

The wise wife realizes that her hus-
band's eyesight is integral to his affection. It is
this point that motivates her *to care for herself*
consistently. How was he, after all, first attracted to you? By what he saw! In the
courtship period, the girl is very careful of her
appearance, knowing it is important to keep

herself attractive. She is also motivated by her love for the young man. She wants to do everything she can to please him. What, then, happens after marriage? Why do we see so many women "go to pot" within a few years of their wedding? They get careless about their makeup and hairstyle, sloppy in their dress, and derelict in their weight-watching. "I'm just so contented in marriage!" is a mighty silly excuse. The object, wife, is to do your dead-level best to keep your *husband* contented in marriage! Pleasing his eyes is an important part of that contentment. You should be as pleasing for him to look at as possible. Why? Because your appearance either insults him or pays him a compliment. Dowdiness says in effect, "You're not worth the effort it takes to stay looking good." Attractiveness says, "You're well worth all the effort!" Depending upon which of those messages you choose, you either subtract from or add to the strength of your love bond. I *know* it's hard to spend time on your own appearance when you have a houseful of small children. I *know* each year of aging makes it harder, but the principle still holds. Will you insult or compliment him by your appearance? The choice is up to you. It's a work of the heart.

The worlds of the heart. God's Word warns, "The heart is deceitful above all things, and desperately wicked: who can know it?" (Jer. 17:9). There is a world of *deceit* in the heart! How else to explain the woman who talks long and loud about submission while all the while she is running the show at home?

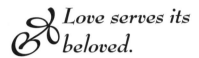

Love serves its beloved.

How else to explain the wife who lets herself look frumpy while claiming deep spirituality? How else to explain ourselves and the contrast between what we yearn to be as wives and what we actually are? The deceitful heart is constantly at work deceiving us about our motivations and our methods in marriage.

There is also a world of *self* in the heart. That world looms large, and its whirling captures far too much of our attention. It distracts from the concentration of love, care, and effort we should expend upon our husbands. Love serves its beloved. Self resists bowing in service. An unlovely world, Self! A world that defies our best efforts at shrinkage—a world that often disguises itself as spirituality, or common sense, or maturity. A world that, though perhaps momentarily conquered, looms large and whole again in the very next moment.

Finally, there is a world of *beauty* available to the heart. It is not a trumped-up, humanly maintained beauty, but rather one bestowed and nurtured by God Himself. It is that heart's world of beauty with which we'll concern ourselves next.

Chapter Seven

A God-Formed Rib

"**And** the Lord God caused a deep sleep to fall upon Adam, and he slept: and he took one of his ribs, and closed up the flesh instead thereof; And the rib, which the Lord God had taken from man, made he a woman, and brought her unto the man" (Genesis 2:21-22). What beautiful simplicity! It's as you and I stray from God's original design that we complicate our lives and corrupt our love. Though Eden lies far behind us, our hearts still echo Satan's whisper, "Hath God said?"

Think back for a moment over the six earlier chapters of this little book. They say nothing of techniques or step-by-step plans for being a better wife. Instead, every consideration could be reduced to *attitudes*—attitudes of mind and heart. Why? Because I firmly believe attitudes form the core of our problems and hold the key to our improvement. As God Himself puts it, "Keep thy heart with all diligence; for out of it are the issues of life" (Proverbs 4:23).

"Keep thy heart." First, we need to keep our hearts in the sense of protecting them. One of the great causes of unhappiness in marriage is the wife's hearkening to the wrong people and things. A mother and/or father, for instance, can cause problems by suggestive phrases such as, "Doesn't it bother you that your husband does so-and-so?" Or "Well, now, I really think that's going too far in the leadership bit, don't you?" Or "Oh my goodness— your father would *never* have done that!"

> *Attitudes hold the key to our improvement.*

Motivated though they be by love and concern for their offspring, parents nevertheless can discolor a wife's attitude toward her unique

marriage and marriage partner. Friends can
likewise get a heart out of kilter. In "sharing"
sessions among married women, for instance,
others' evaluations and revelations can cause
uneasy questioning as to whether, by comparison, her marriage really measures up. If she is
a working wife, a Christian woman can come
to feel that she is the one whose marriage is
lacking as the unsaved around her babble of
extramarital flirtations, 50/50 marriages, and
multiple "affairs." But the woman working
outside the home is not alone in needing to
protect her heart. Destructive forces invade
the home as well. Consider the unholy content of newspapers, magazines, books, and
TV! If she's unwise enough to take in any of
these proclamations and insinuations, a
woman can grow resentful, restless, and rebellious. Those "3 Rs" add up to *flunking out* as a
godly wife!

We also need to protect our hearts
against ourselves. Although redeemed by the
precious blood of the Lord Jesus Christ, we
still have a sinful nature, a nature alarmingly
alive and well. The "flesh" within would
squeeze our hearts all out of shape until they
were narrow with self-interest, shallow in
compassion and understanding, bloated with

pride, and broad with stubbornness. Those distortions strongly contrast with the "meek and quiet spirit" to which we're enjoined in I Peter 3:4.

Second, we need to keep our hearts in the sense of preserving them. When something is preserved, it is specially prepared, sealed, and set apart. That's a good picture of the right kind of wifely heart. Its special preparation takes place in the prayer closet, where the woman spends time alone with the Lord each day, reading His Word and praying. Without that all-important, special preparation, the spoilage in her heart will show itself throughout the day in her attitude and actions toward her husband. The link between the spiritual and the marital never ceases to amaze me. There is all the difference in the world in my wifing on days when I'm in close, obedient fellowship with the Lord and those days when I'm out of sorts with Him. Human love and willpower are never enough. It must be God's power working through me that carries me to marital success. According to Philippians 2:13, "For it is God which worketh in you both to will and to do of his good pleasure."

The second aspect of a preserved heart is its sealing. To my mind, that is a daily transaction the Christian woman makes by asking God to empower her with His Holy Spirit for this day, this moment, of her marriage. A convicting picture comes through clearly in Ecclesiastes 10:1—"Dead flies cause the ointment of the apothecary to send forth a stinking savour: so doth a little folly him that is in reputation for wisdom and honour." Only the Holy Spirit's seal will keep out the "flies" of sinful attitudes Satan tries to drop into our hearts.

Third, the preserved heart must be set apart. In other words, the Christian wife needs to dedicate herself to the Lord's will and service each day. Somehow, we have fallen into the error of thinking wholehearted spiritual commitment is only for preachers and missionaries. Not so. When God wrote through the apostle Paul, "Present your bodies a living sacrifice," He was directing the instruction to the lay people of the church in Rome. Consistent setting apart unto the Lord reminds the wife whose she is and whom she serves; it gives her a moment-by-moment sense of responsibility to God.

Ribbing Him Rightly

"With all diligence." That is a pivotal phrase for our success as wives. I've found in talking to Christian women in groups and individually that rather than not knowing the scriptural principles of godly wifing, the problem lies in not doing what we know! It would be much easier if we could sit back, fold our hands, and have God magically preserve our hearts, eliminating from them all foreign defiling elements. But that's not the way the Lord works. Remember the phrase "We then, as workers together with him" (II Corinthians 6:1). Yes, God does convict and He does empower—but He also demands that we actively participate. *"With all diligence."* That sounds like hard, day-in, day-out work, doesn't it? And so it is. Diligence: the determined use of energy. Without such effort, our hearts will be left exposed to corruptive "dead flies" of attitude.

I have found the most effective way of diligently keeping my heart is to meditate on Scripture. In our domestic lives there is a great deal of time when we don't have to concentrate on what we're doing: ironing, scrubbing, dusting, and so on. Have you ever noticed how self-pity, discouragement, and/or a generally lousy attitude can set in during those busy-body-but-free-mind times? That's because a detached mind takes the path of least resistance—downward. When an automobile is parked on an incline, we set the wheels against the curbing to prevent a runaway. The identical principle applies to our hearts. We are to be "bringing into captivity every thought to the obedience of Christ" (II Corinthians 10:5). By meditating upon God's Word, we not only "set the wheels" against the pull of that decline, but we also experience God's *reversal* of the decline! Our prayer can be like Solomon's: "That he may incline our hearts unto him, to walk in all his ways, and to keep his commandments, and his statutes, and his judgments, which he commanded our fathers" (I Kings 8:58).

Meditation is simple but strategic. Take a single verse from your day's Bible reading. Write it on a card or memorize it so that you can have it with you throughout the day. In moments of nonconcentration, think about the verse. Ask yourself questions about the passage. Seek illustrations for it from your own surroundings and activities. Explore the varying shades of meaning by emphasizing different words. Talk to the Lord, asking Him to show you exactly how to apply the verse to your personal needs. What riches there are in meditation—not only for ourselves but also for those around us as we are challenged and changed by God's Word! As I Timothy 4:15 puts it, we are to "meditate upon these things; give thyself wholly to them; that thy profiting may appear to all."

"Keep thy heart with all diligence: for out of it are the issues of life." These words make it clear that our actions and reactions issue from the heart. My husband's grandfather had a saying that succinctly states the case: "No doubt the trouble is with *you*." I've proved that uncomfortable truth repeatedly in my home setting. Haven't you? I get all out of joint, then in "explaining" (excusing) myself, I point to my husband, or the children, or my in-laws, or the schedule, or the circumstances, or the physical setting, but nine and nine-tenths times out of ten the *real* cause is right in my own heart.

> *What riches there are in meditation.*

Let's take the example of an argument. A husband makes a remark that irritates or hurts his wife. She responds in kind, and soon the two are arguing loudly or freezing one another in icy silence. Despite attempts at self-

justification in such situations, the Bible reminds us that "only by pride cometh con-
tention" (Proverbs 13:10). As if that weren't
enough to point the finger of responsibility
back where it belongs, we're reminded in
Proverbs 15:1 that "a soft answer turneth
away wrath." Now certainly, the wife doesn't
bear all the responsibility of upsets and
downturns in the home: a husband shoulders
a good deal of it too. But we women act and
react in ways that either aggravate or improve
the situation.

There is a little-noticed but interesting passage in Proverbs 27. It's the nine-
teenth verse: "As in water face answereth to
face, so the heart of man to man." Do you get
the picture? Like a still pond, we *mirror* one
another's attitudes. Anger breeds anger, nastiness encourages nastiness—and so it goes
unless one of the two "brings a new face" into
the situation. Let me share a personal example with you.

One Friday evening our domestic bliss
threatened to explode. The week had been a
long, hard one for my husband. But instead
of coming home to expectations of weekend .
relaxation, he became part of a whirlwind of
preparations for a Boy Scout father-son

camp-out. There was banging and clanging from one end of the house to the other. The faster Bob worked, the more frustrating everything became. It was impossible to find needed items. The son part of the camp-out had forgotten to pre-assemble equipment. The only bedding available for my six-foot-four-inch husband was a five-foot-six-inch sleeping bag. All of us were getting into a high state of agitation by the time Bob stood amid the equipment-mounded family room and snorted disgustedly that this was *some* way to have to spend a *cold* weekend! At that point, my "decline" pointed toward husband-bashing with the Coleman stove. But the Lord's inward reminder about soft answers changed the incline. I went over to my exhausted, frustrated husband, put my arms around his neck, and, laughing, smothered him with kisses, while telling him what a sweet husband and father he is. For a moment the rigidity of anger held. Then Bob sputtered into laughter. The whole situation was calmed as I "brought a new face" into it. Unfortunately, for that one positive instance, I could cite many in which my "old face" shamefully escalated anger.

"For out of it are the issues of life." .
The heart is the source for every aspect of our
living. That concept makes one squirm with
conviction. It's so much nicer to blame anyone or anything rather than facing up to our
personal responsibility. According to this
verse, the source of our performance (and
problems) as wives is our own heart.

The truth of this heart-source principle has been made clear to me over and over
again in counseling sessions with women.
Some crumble under the pressure of ordinary,
everyday living. On the other end of the spec-
trum are those wives whose Christlike radi-
ance has grown brighter through years of great
domestic difficulties. I think particularly of
Christian women married to unsaved, alcoholic men. Their lives—even in imagina-
tion—make most of ours look like Utopia! I
remember one woman who was magnetically
lovely, trim, graceful, beautifully groomed,
and *radiant* in her Christianity. Yet her life was
a constant struggle with an intemperate husband. He not only rejected the Lord himself,
but he also begrudged her the encouragement
and joy of Christian fellowship. He frequently
forbade her to go to church, ladies' meetings,
and so on. Yet that woman walked in the most

obvious spiritual victory! She is a lovely spiritual magnet—and sooner or later her man must be drawn irresistibly to the Christ she so beautifully mirrors.

Another lady told me with quiet joy of the marvelous change in her formerly alcoholic husband since his salvation. She went on to say, "After he was saved, someone asked my husband what finally drew him to the Lord. He answered that it was my treating him like a king all through the first eleven drunken years of our marriage." That woman's *heart* was right, and the life issuing from the heart was likewise right, ultimately bringing her husband to the Lord Jesus.

For those of you dear Christian women with unsaved or spiritually disobedient husbands, I would prayerfully urge you to burn I Peter 3:1 into the fiber of your being: "Likewise, ye wives, be in subjection to your own husbands; that, if any obey not the word, they also may without the word be won by the conversation of the wives."

Notice the first word: "Likewise." That refers to the instructions preceding it, a passage dealing with servants of unpleasant, unfair masters. Such servants are told to be as cheerfully and faithfully obedient as if they

served the best of masters. So then—likewise—wives of difficult husbands are to be as
cheerfully and faithfully submissive as if they
had the world's best husbands.

Second, look at the word "conversation." It does not mean "speech." Instead, the
meaning is "manner of
life," so the thought is,
"You wives of husbands
who are not what they
ought to be spiritually
(doesn't *that* cover a lot
of territory!) are never-

Keeping her heart right is the hardest thing any wife has to do.

theless to do a godly job of wifing so that he
who will not heed the Word (or any words)
can be won by the *life* of his wife." The wife in
a difficult marriage should not badger her
man (nagging him to go to church, acting like
a martyr if he won't, banging him over the
head with Scripture clubs, leaving devotional
booklets open to appropriate pages on his
bedside table, writing a Bible verse on the
bottom of his cereal bowl) but rather should
be quiet and live!

Heart attitude. It seems pretty simple
when they're just words on paper, but keeping
her heart right is the hardest thing any wife
has to do. Knowing that the heart is the

source of her life's stream, Satan tirelessly
tries to pollute it. How many of the following
pollutants has he introduced into your attitude just in the past twenty-four hours: complaint, resentment, self-pity, criticism, anger,
irritation, impatience, and bitterness? No
wonder our marriages suffer!

This talk of pollution would be thor-
oughly discouraging without the assurance
that Jesus Christ possesses the antipollutant.
He delights to do what no amount of
self-help or positive thinking can ever accomplish, and that is to dredge and renew the
source of our life streams. But we need to be
aware that this transaction must occur every
day—and sometimes several times a day. We
must cry repeatedly, like the penitent David,
"Create in me a clean heart, O God; and
renew a right spirit within me" (Psalm 51:10).

As we do so, we can claim the assurance voiced by the apostle Paul in II Timothy
4:18—"And the Lord shall deliver me from
every evil work, and will preserve me unto his
heavenly kingdom."

But what attitudes, specifically, should
characterize our hearts? In a nutshell, they're
the fruit of the Spirit: love, joy, peace, longsuffering, gentleness, goodness, faith, meek-

ness, temperance (Galatians 5:22-23). Any
one of us who has lived past the age of five
recognizes that those are not natural characteristics. They are supernatural. Hence the
necessity to live moment by moment in responsive fellowship with the Lord. Part of our
responsiveness is our *positive* force of *will*: deciding we want to do and *will do* the godly
thing in each situation. Consistently choosing
the positive reaction is of vital importance—
not only in a specific situation but also in setting the overall, habitual tone of married life.

Listen to the conversation of
Christian wives in unguarded moments when
they're not trying to impress anyone. The
thing that comes through loud and clear is
negativism. Words like "can't," "difficult,"
"tired," "dislike," and "impossible" far out-
weigh positive words, don't they? Now moni-
tor your own thought patterns for a day or
two. You'll probably find the same. *Negativism.*
How antithetical our negative thought patterns are to all the positives of God's character and Word! If only we could realize that we
will never enjoy the roses of life if we're always
looking at the thorns!

Since it's obvious that our heart focus
must not be negative, what specific positives

should shape our vision? Most of us need to make considerable adjustment in the areas of Savior, self, and service. I believe the most valuable single sight-adjuster in all those areas is gratitude. We should have unending, unstinting *gratitude* to Jesus Christ for His gift of eternal life and abundant temporal life; genuine gratitude for the God-planned, unique persons we are (including all so-called flaws); and, finally, wholehearted gratitude for our service—our important service to God that is clothed in the mundane disguise of marriage.

> *Marriage for a Christian woman is, ultimately, a ministry.*

Marriage for a Christian woman is, ultimately, a ministry, and for that reason each successful wife must pray and determine to be a God-formed rib. How do we set about this process of molding and changing? By wholeheartedly committing ourselves to the ministry of right wifing and the shaping God will perform in answer to our desires. We must irrevocably commit ourselves, no matter how hurtful and discouraging the project may prove to be. Our focus must be upon Him whom we serve. The required single-minded

spirit is beautifully expressed in Psalm 27:4:
"One thing have I desired of the Lord, that
will I seek after; that I may dwell in the house
of the Lord all the days of my life, to behold
the beauty of the Lord, and to inquire in his
temple." As we dwell daily in His presence,
gaze upon His face, and take our inquiries
and injuries to His throne, we will begin to re-
flect Him. Such is the molding we must have
if we are ever to attain the high and holy call-
ing of godly wifing.

Consider the powerful message of
Proverbs 24:3-4: "Through wisdom is an
house builded; and by understanding it is established: and by knowledge shall the chambers be filled with all precious and pleasant
riches." These verses clearly enunciate the
ministry of marriage.

First, we're told that godly wisdom is
foundational to a home. A strong marriage,
then, must stand on spiritual concrete. Yet so
many Christian wives substitute "legal right,"
"our love for each other," "my opposition to
divorce," or any number of other things. One
and all, they fail as foundation material.

Second, godly wisdom is formative. In
every moment and day of a marriage, the wife
is being either constructive or destructive

(Proverbs 14:1). We need God-given insight to help us know the difference. Some attitudes and actions are destructive without our recognizing them as such. God alone is Creator and Builder; Satan and our old natures are destroyers. Moreover, "the wisdom of this world is foolishness with God" (I Corinthians 3:19a). Between our destructive natures and our foolish minds, our homes stand in jeopardy.

And finally, godly wisdom is filling. The home where God's will and way are active isn't just a thing of flooring and walls; it is a structure filled with the unique happiness that family warmth produces. Blessed indeed is the home divine wisdom founds, forms, and fills. "Through wisdom is an house builded; and by understanding it is established: And by knowledge shall the chambers be filled with all precious and pleasant riches" (Proverbs 24:3-4).

You and I are *promised* God's wisdom and His power for the all-important ministry of marriage. James 1:5 "If any of you lack wisdom, let him ask of God, that giveth to all men liberally, and upbraideth not; and it shall be given him." And Jeremiah 33:3 "Call unto me, and I will answer thee, and shew thee great and mighty things, which thou knowest not."

The choice is clear: the mire of weakness, frustration, hostility, and defeat, or the miracle of power, joy, unity, and victory. Just as God in Eden's day created woman from man's rib, so in this day He alone can rightly create man's rib from woman! In Proverbs 19:14b we have it clearly pointed out that "a prudent wife is from the Lord." O that you and I might be malleable in His hands!

ॐ

Chapter Eight

Letter

Mr. Husband
101 Domestic Lane
Anywhere, USA

Dear Husband,

 After writing an entire book to your
wife, I'm writing just this letter to you for the
sake of balance.

 I have listened to and read letters from
many, many Christian women across America.
The thing that always strikes me most forcibly
is the *deep desire God's women have to be the
wives their husbands want and need!* They are
quick to recognize and admit their failures.

Their determination in the face of difficulties sometimes deserves a medal of honor! But a wife *cannot* build a marriage alone.

My purpose is not to instruct, but rather to appeal to you. That appeal is three-fold.

&Please know your wife

&Please love your wife

&Please value your wife

Please know your wife. First Peter 3:7 contains the phrase "dwell with them (wives) according to knowledge." Marriage it-self provides your dwelling with your wife; God and you must work together in order for you to know your wife in the right way. Al-though she comes in the basic packaging shared by all women, your wife is nevertheless unlike any other woman. She's one of God's human "snowflakes"—unique! The unity God intends for marriage goes far beyond the physical. Hearts, minds, and spirits should also merge into one. One of the prerequisites for such blending is knowing one another. In the preceding pages, your wife has been urged to make a detailed study of the unique person you are. The same or a similar study of her would be a worthwhile undertaking for you. One of the great disappointments to a woman after marriage is her husband's taking her for granted. By rekindling an interest in really knowing her, you can add a new dimension of joy to your wife's life.

Your wife is a woman. Silly to have to say that, isn't it? But "woman" signifies an entire being quite unlike yours. Your wife's mind doesn't operate like yours. She sees things from a near-at-hand viewpoint; she's strong on details, but weak on an overall or long-range view. Her mental mechanism is much more closely connected to her emotional motor than yours is. She reasons subjectively, not objectively. She more often sees things in human terms than in a strictly logical, cause-and-effect, worse-or-better light. Too, she has a sense that is beyond reason—intuition. Mysterious as it may seem to a husband, the female mind is God's creation just as is the male mind. The mental differences between you and your wife aren't meant to frustrate, but to fulfill. Together you can have a wonderful mental wholeness.

Take into account the physical differences between you. God calls woman "the weaker vessel." Chances are your wife doesn't

have the stamina you possess. She needs more
sleep than you. When she doesn't get it, her
whole psychological, emotional, and physical
self can run down very quickly. My husband
and I know a couple who had to learn this
basic distinction the hard way. A busy pastor,
the man for years expected his wife to keep
the same hours and shoulder church burdens
as he. Her health took a disastrous downturn.
The attending physician told the husband in
no uncertain terms that his wife could not
function as an assistant pastor. Only then
were common-sense adjustments made to
protect the wife. The changes, by the way,
made both husband and wife happier and
more effective.

Because she is unique, your wife possesses certain personality characteristics that
you alone may know. It has always seemed humorous to me to read books or hear lectures
that categorize people. Oh yes, there are some
vague general likenesses, but simply to pigeonhole people according to "type" leaves the
greater part of any individual hanging outside
the pigeonhole! Don't try to stick a psychological or personality label on your wife. Labels
make people "whats." Instead, why not really
observe her and ask God to make you sensi-

tive to who she is. Her unique combination of ingredients makes her an unendingly interesting study subject. And the more you understand her, the more you can appreciate her. In turn, your heightened interest and appreciation will make your wife glow. But it's extremely important that in your wife study you accept her as she is—a unique creation of God. Displeasure or disdain will crush her heart.

Please love your wife. Ephesians 5:25 conveys the Scripture's command to do so. It is a truism that women are responders. A wife very much wants to be a "zucchini bread" mate. (Ask her to share the joke with you or see the story in Chapter Six.) But her successful fulfillment of that desire largely depends on what you give her to respond to. Proverbs 27:19 says, "As in water face answereth to face, so the heart of man to man." That's particularly true in the husband-wife relationship. A loved woman is a loving woman. And what red-blooded American male doesn't want warm, sweet love from his wife? The hitch usually comes in the matter of communication and interpretation. When asked, "Do you love your wife?" almost every man will answer with a quick, firm "Yes!" Yet there are

Ribbing Him Rightly

Christian women who have whispered broken-
heartedly to me, "I don't think my husband
really loves me." Obviously, the train carrying
the message of love is not reaching its intended goal! Something is making it jump the
track before it reaches the correct station.
Think about some of the logs that may be lit-
tering the tracks.

Log Number One: Love assumed instead of expressed. Many men consider their
material support of a wife to be proof positive
of love for her. And it is. But *proof* is a cold
word. Money and houses can't hug a woman.
A wife needs her man to *say* "I love you."
Those are the sweetest words ever to enter the
female ear. And the ear craves their repeated
hearing. It may seem strange to your logical
male mind, but a woman would gladly sacrifice material proofs of love for verbally expressed love! A wife is very much like a plant:
she needs sunlight. That sunlight is her husband's spoken love. Without it, she can wilt
and die. Extreme? Not really. God's main instruction to husbands is "Love your wives." He
who made women knows the extent of their
need. So—please—roll that log of silence off
the track and send the train on through with
every turn of the wheels saying "I love you . . .

I love you . . . I love you. . . ." Say it in sun-
shine. Say it in rain. Say it in prosperity. Say
it in adversity. Say it in gladness. Say it in
sorrow. Say it when she's an angel. Say it
when she's a witch. *Speak* your love!

Log Number Two: Love demonstrated
practically rather than personally. Just as
within every male breast there lurks a little
boy who likes airplanes, trucks, or sports, so
too within every female breast there lives a
little girl. She most probably does *not* like airplanes, trucks, or sports. But she *does* like
"sweet" things: a mushy greeting card, a sentimental song or story, a kitten, flowers, candy,
jewelry, or lacy lingerie. A man often calls
such things "impractical." A woman, while she
admits that they are, in the strictest sense, impractical, will point out that they are important *because* they're impractical! They touch
her heart. The life of a wife is, necessarily, a
highly practical existence. She is mired in
down-to-earth things like errands, sweeping,
diaper changing, dusting, nose blowing, scrubbing, puppy training, cooking, window washing, and so on. When you think about it, most
of the things a wife does (including holding a
job outside the home) are for the sake of *others*. All the while, the little girl inside her

stands shyly in the shadows, silently longing for the magic of a sentimental "something" for *her alone*. Please, won't you tune up your sensitivity to that little girl within your wife? At gift-giving time and for surprises between times, choose the lovely over the labor-saving, the personal over the practical, and the sweet over the sensible. The train of love will move forward double-time.

Log Number Three: Love commandeering rather than wooing. Your wife approaches physical lovemaking from the opposite direction you do. Yours is the dominant, *taking* role; hers is the subordinate, *giving* one. Your motivation is primarily *physical*, hers *emotional*. You are stimulated by *sight*, she by *touch*. It's only as those opposites are truly joined that physical union can be all God intends it should be. Here, too, I can assure you your wife wants to be the free, responsive, exciting partner you desire. But she *can't* reach that ideal alone. God made her a responder. After years of listening to women's marital woes, I'm convinced that clinical details are *not* what's needed. Instead, the essential masculine ingredient for bringing beauty to the marriage bed is respectful recognition.

First *respect* your mate's inhibitions
and timidity. A girl is reared with an emphasis
on purity and modesty. That's as it should be.
But it is very difficult for her, upon marriage,
suddenly to change her whole emotional orientation. Also, there may be experiences in
your wife's background that have left her
emotionally scarred. Whatever "programming"
she brings into marriage, the husbandly cure
is *not* "Ah, knock it off—we're *married!* You're
silly to be shy!" Instead, there should be sym-
pathetic understanding of her inhibitions and
then a gentle winning of her change in outlook. Because of your wife's inhibition, she
may experience difficulty in her exhibition.
What she needs is your gentle, patient leadership in love. Coach her in those physical
demonstrations of affection you crave, and
urge her to do the same for you. Please, *please*
don't express (either verbally or facially) disappointment in your wife's bedroom behavior.
Nor should you *ever* ask of her acts of perversity. Doing that can put her into a lifelong
deep freeze. Also, respect her enough to skip
any sermonizing! If you feel a sermon is absolutely necessary, go to I Corinthians 13 and
let the Lord preach *you* a sermon—about real
love. A woman must know she can trust her

man. Part of that trust springs from his respect for her.

Second give your wife respectful *recognition*. The different perspective from which your wife approaches bedroom behavior doesn't mean that hers is either inferior or unreasonable. It is the way God and her upbringing made her. Some wives tell me that their husbands simply ignore the feminine psyche entirely, charging into and through the time of physical union with about as much sensitivity as Attila the Hun. Such men are to be pitied. Their callousness is leaving *both themselves and their wives out in the cold of incompleteness.* How much wiser and more rewarding is the loving husband's acknowledgement of his wife's physical/emotional makeup and his tender winning her over! Let me share with you some of the "turn-offs" women mention as influencing their bedroom mood:

✂ The electric-switch/rush-hour lover. The too-sudden, out-of-the-blue, "Let's hop into bed" approach usually leaves a woman totally unmoved—or else moved away from her husband's advances! The sense of hurry works against a woman's responsiveness.

❧ The "arena" lover. He may be able to enjoy intimacy while the house is full of wide-awake kids, relatives, and so on. She can't.

Conversely, there are things that help make your wife positively responsive:

❧ Expression/demonstration of love throughout the day. One of the most effective ways you can make your love a day-long thing is by consistent acts of courtesy and affection. Treat your wife like a lady—she will love you for it! Fill her day with demonstrated affection: holding her hand, giving her a quick hug, touching her face, and so on. A bedroom only lover makes a woman feel both cheated and cheap.

❧ Choice of an appropriate, relaxed time for both of you. For example, your morning is only a matter of getting dressed, shaved, and fed. Hers is a major, demanding production involving house, kids, food, and self. A sense of privacy is very important to a woman. The possibility of being overheard or of someone walking in on you makes a wife a bundle of nonpassionate nerves.

• Consideration of her emotional makeup. Restraining your emotional mechanism for the sake of protecting her sensitivities and awakening her responsiveness speaks volumes to a wife about the Christlikeness and depth of your love.

Log Number Four: Love with wandering eyes. A woman's greatest emotional need is for security. If a husband looks at, comments about, and compliments other women, he systematically strips away his wife's sense of security. Whatever his protestations to the contrary, a man's wandering eyes tell his wife she's not loved as she should be—*exclusively!*

Everywhere today, we see Satan breaking Christian homes. Your best insurance, humanly speaking, against his destroying your home is your Christlike, demonstrated, considerate, exclusive love for your wife.

Please value your wife. Proverbs 31:10 points out that a godly wife is a treasure. But overhearing men speak about and to their wives and listening to women pour out their burdened, unhappy hearts, it's easy to see that far too often the proper value is not placed on wives. There are specific areas in which you need to value your wife. First, value her mental capacity. It's the man of small, weak character and spirituality who lives with the attitude, "Now, I'm runnin' this show, and you just keep your mouth shut, woman!" The husband who spends time in God's Word and who also exercises common sense knows his wife's thinking is an important asset to him. Your wife is your "details man," your intellectual accountant as it were. Her complementary thinking can save you untold headaches and heartaches. She can also be of great help to you through her intuitive reactions. She is able to evaluate character, attitudes, and intentions. Please, if your wife doesn't have as much formal education as you or she doesn't occupy your intellectual plane, don't put her down as a dummy. Education? She probably gave up continuing her education in order to help you finish! And "intellectual planes" are pretty unimportant and contrived, anyway. Whatever your wife's level of formal education or IQ, you can be sure that her solid, practical thinking will fill up gaps in yours.

Second, value her emotional structure. *Emotionalism* is a word often snorted by husbands as they disgustedly react to or complain about their wives. But, again, by selling his wife short because of her emotional makeup, many a husband loses a tremendous asset.

Ribbing Him Rightly

Although there is no really accurate way to assign percentages to emotional composition, let's say just for the sake of illustration that a man is 75 percent logic and 25 percent emotion, while his wife is 75 percent emotion and 25 percent logic. Obviously those differences can cause fireworks and disaster. But they don't *have* to. They can also bring fulfillment and dimension. Mental acuity alone is cold. Emotion alone is inflammatory. By superimposing the wife's emotional/logical makeup on the husband's, or vice versa, both are fully *covered* and *balanced* in the whole! Marvelous interlocking planned by God, isn't there? Too, think how your wife's emotional structure adds value to your life each day. It gives her the tenderness to comfort and encourage you. It makes her a gentle, loving mother. It creates the "spark" that kindles your passion. It gives her a "sixth sense" about people and situations that can safeguard you. In short, your wife's emotional capacity adds dimension to your life!

Third, value her womanly role. Most of your wife's innumerable accomplishments are performed in an unsung, unseen manner and place. While you're out battling in the professional, business, or laboring world, she's battling too, but without the glow and encouragement of publicity and social interaction that you enjoy. Like yours, her labors are physically demanding. Whether or not she has an outside job, she *works*—as you do, but longer. While you're relaxing with the evening newspaper, she's fixing dinner or cleaning up or ironing or getting the children bathed or otherwise going on with her labors. Like you, she carries heavy responsibilities: the testimony of a neat, clean home; the physical/mental/emotional welfare of your children. Like you, she takes her job seriously. She's always working for greater efficiency, less expense, increased effectiveness. Like you, she knows that her ultimate accountability is to God. Yet all those "like you's" are carried on in a far smaller, far more restricted sphere than your activities. There are unique, often unrecognized pressures on her existence and performance.

- *She's under attack.* Magazines, newspapers, and TV are constantly telling her she's a dupe and a dope to center her life on you.

- *She's lonely.* The busyness of her life and the weight and nature of her responsibilities cut her off from social involvement.

❧ *She's bored.* Her job is characterized by ceaseless repetition in every area. Even if she works outside the home, chances are her job is repetitious—as, for instance, in clerical work.

You make the difference between her role being a job or a joy. You do so by the value you place on her and the commendation you give her! In human terms, you and you alone can relieve the pressures that grind her down each day. *You* can provide her escape from those same three special pressure areas.

❧ *You can counter the attack.* Tell her and show her that who she is and what she is doing are essential to you, that you recognize her contribution to your life as your greatest asset. Also, encourage her in things that make her feel good about herself.

❧ *You can release her from loneliness.* Talk to her! Let her see into your day, your tasks, your burdens, your blessings. Listen to her! Take a real, not a condescending, interest in her doings—and also in her feelings.

  You can relieve her boredom. Break the
routine for her now and then. Take her
out for lunch. Whisk her to a nearby city
for an afternoon of window shopping.
Baby-sit for an evening so she can take a
night class or go visit a friend. Arrange
for your mother to keep the children;
then take your wife to a nice motel for
dinner and overnight. Do any and many
little things you know will surprise and
please her.

   Proverbs 12:4 declares, "A virtuous
woman is a crown to her husband." A king
values his crown. He wears it gratefully,
proudly. *It is the visible symbol of his station and
power.* That's exactly what your wife is to you.
She adorns you. She validates your person
and position. Do you rightly *value* and *cherish*
her?

   Sincerely yours,

Beneth Peters Jones

STUDY GUIDE

꽃

Chapter One
Aye, There's the Rib!

Memorize It

Genesis 2:18

"And the Lord God said, It is not good
that the man should be alone; I will make him
an help meet for him."

Answer It

Based on God's declaration after the creation of woman, a wife is seen as a magnifier:
she completes and expands her husband. List
several ways that you complete your husband.
How do you expand him?

As a rib, you should support and protect
him. What aspect of that support is most difficult for you? Give a recent incident in
which you protected your husband.

Study It

Read Genesis 1:26-31, Genesis 2:18-25,
I Corinthians 11:8-9, and Ephesians 5:22-
28. How are you a unique creation of God?
What are some of your unique purposes?

ℬ

Chapter Two
Ribbing a Man

Memorize It

Ephesians 5:23-24

"For the husband is the head of the wife, even as Christ is the head of the church: and he is the saviour of the body. Therefore as the church is subject unto Christ, so let the wives be to their own husbands in every thing."

Answer It

Genesis 5:2 states, "Male and female created he [God] them." God intended two different but complementary beings. Give a recent situation in which you've complemented (completed) your husband.

Five differences between men and women are discussed in this chapter: thinking patterns, life focus, neatness/sensitivity, maturity and flexibility. Choose one difference that is especially challenging to you. List several ways that you can work on that challenge.

What should a wife do with the "flaws" she sees in her husband?

Study It

Using a concordance, look up every reference to woman or wife in the book of Proverbs. Make a list of positive and negative characteristics (e.g., Proverbs 12:4—a crown versus rottenness in his bones).

ॐ

Chapter Three
Exclusive Ribs, Inc.

Memorize It

Psalm 139:14

"I will praise thee; for I [and my husband] am fearfully and wonderfully made: marvellous are thy works; and that my soul knoweth right well."

Answer It

What is the only way to "rib" your husband properly and adequately?

List a character quality in your husband that initially attracted you to him.

Give two specific ways that you can make your husband the center of your focus this week.

Study It

Read a chapter from the Song of Solomon, noting the wife's verbal admiration for her husband. Also note the husband's response to the praise and to his wife.

꽃⬋

Chapter Four
Of Ribs and Ears

Memorize It

Ephesians 4:29

"Let no corrupt communication proceed
out of your mouth, but that which is good to
the use of edifying, that it may minister grace
unto the hearers."

Answer It

Communication is essential to marriage. What does Proverbs 18:13 say about communication?

What warnings does James 1 give about the tongue?

What is the key to right communication in a Christian marriage?

Study It

The Bible has much to say about communication. Using a concordance and focusing on the Book of Proverbs, do a word study on one of the following: *word/words, mouth, speaks/speaketh, hear/heareth, or answer.*

Chapter Five
Rock-Ribbed Support

Memorize It

Proverbs 18:14

"The spirit of a man will sustain his infirmity; but a wounded spirit who can bear?"

Answer It

What is one of the most important purposes a wife can fulfill?

How can you be supportive of your husband in each of the following areas:
- verbal encouragement
- admiration for personal qualities
- commendation for accomplishments
- reassurance in disappointment
- sympathy in failure

According to II Corinthians 1:3-4, what
is a natural consequence of our going to God
for comfort?

Study It

A woman must depend on the Word of God to be a godly wife. What common theme is found in the following verses: Ephesians 1:17-19; Ephesians 3:20; Ephesians 6:10; Philippians 4:13, 19; Colossians 1:10-11?

ॐ

Chapter Six
Ribs—Cage for His Heart

Memorize It

Proverbs 31:11

"The heart of her husband doth safely trust in her, so that he shall have no need of spoil."

Answer It

What is the most important part of a man that is given to his wife's care?

List five specific ways you can protect your husband's heart.

Look up the word *jealous* in a dictionary. Choose one meaning that is destructive to a marriage. Choose one that is necessary to a marriage.

List several characteristics of love according to I Corinthians 13:4-8.

Study It

Study Proverbs 31:10-31 and Titus 2:4-5. Make a list of the characteristics of a godly wife.

ॐ

Chapter Seven
A God-Formed Rib

Memorize It

Proverbs 4:23

"Keep thy heart with all diligence; for out of it are the issues of life."

Answer It

What forms the core of our problems and holds the key to our improvement?

What are the "3 Rs" that add up to flunking out as a godly wife?

According to I Timothy 4:15, what is one benefit of meditation?

Proverbs 24:3-4 describes godly wisdom. What three principles can be applied to the ministry of marriage?

What is the biblical definition of conversation? According to I Peter 1:15, what should describe our conversation?

Study It

The attitudes that a godly woman should have are summarized in the fruit of the Spirit given in Galatians 5:22. How can focusing on each aspect of the fruit of the Spirit change your responses to your husband?